LEONARDO
DA VINCI
PUZZLES

LEONARDO
DA VINCI
PUZZLES

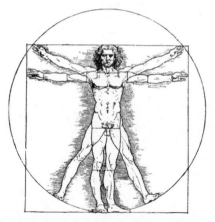

CREATIVE CHALLENGES
INSPIRED BY THE MASTER OF
THE RENAISSANCE

Dr Gareth Moore

This edition published in 2022 by Arcturus Publishing Limited
26/27 Bickels Yard, 151–153 Bermondsey Street,
London SE1 3HA

AD008188NT

Printed in the UK

Contents

Introduction

If there was ever a man ahead of his time, it was Leonardo da Vinci. Although he is most famous for his iconic works of art—the Mona Lisa most of all—Leonardo da Vinci came up with countless ideas for mechanical devices and inventions throughout his life, as well as solutions to some of the most complex puzzles of the natural world. Born in the 15th century, his work spanned an extraordinary range of topics, with botany, anatomy, mathematics, sculpture, physics, astronomy, engineering, and meteorology all touched upon in his writings and designs. He was also a prolific writer, and indeed most of what we know of Leonardo's myriad ideas comes from his own notes, with thousands of pages still surviving that detail the many inventions and artistic masterpieces he worked on.

Leonardo da Vinci made copious sketches and provided detailed measurements for many of his inventions, and so in turn most of the puzzles in this book really do refer to some real engineering or scientific question that he grappled with during his lifetime and documented in his extraordinary body of written and visual work. That said, it is not known whether any of them were physically built during his lifetime, so the puzzles themselves are of course entirely fictional.

Each of the many conundrums, problems and puzzles in this book is designed to have just one, unique answer, and will require nothing more than a sharp pencil—and a sharp mind—to be solved. All the necessary information will be given on the page in front of you, with no additional knowledge required beyond occasionally some basic mathematical skills. Thinking logically should be all that is needed to help you reach the correct conclusion in each case. A knowledge of Leonardo or his works might occasionally help point you in the right direction in your search for a solution, but this is never required. Full solutions are provided at the back of the book for you to confirm your answers.

Although the puzzles can be tackled in any order you like, some themes do recur and the puzzles are arranged in a deliberate order so that they will work best if read through in page order—and note that once or twice a later puzzle will include content that would provide a strong hint to the solution of an earlier puzzle, if read out of order. And if you get stuck on a puzzle—and sometimes you will—then put it aside and come back to it later when inspiration may eventually strike or try asking a friend to check the solution and give you a hint.

So, prepare to be transported to the Renaissance world of Leonardo da Vinci, and to tackle some of the same intellectual challenges that he himself may once have encountered.

Walking on Water 1

Leonardo da Vinci was working in his workshop on a new invention which would allow the wearer to walk on water. He had developed three prototypes, all three of which were a type of wooden platform that any wearer could attach to their shoe, the idea being that they could then set out to walk across whichever river or lake they wished.

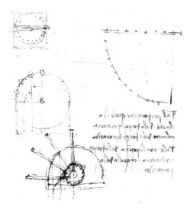

Each prototype model had been made with a different type of wood, and had a different number of coats of varnish applied in an attempt to establish waterproofing. All of the models were quite different in shape: one was very long, one was very wide, and one was very small.

- The beechwood model was not the triple-varnished one
- The widest model was made of olive wood
- The smallest model had two coats of varnish
- The model with a single coat of varnish was also the longest one
- The model made of pine was made before making the longest model

Leonardo suspected that the widest model would be the most successful. What wood had he made it with, and how many coats of varnish had been applied?

Dipping Point

Leonardo da Vinci was in his studio with several of his students. On this particular day he was holding a workshop on the art of creating paint hues by blending precious pigments sent from abroad. Each blend of pigment was carefully measured to create the perfect shade for one of his masterpieces.

Leonardo had two paint pots on the table in front of him: one a deep red, and the other a deep blue. He used a spoon to take a specific amount of the red paint and tip it into the blue pot, and swirled the new mixture until it was roughly mixed. With the same spoon, he then took from the new mixed pot exactly the same amount of paint as before, and tipped it into the red pot, so that both pots now contained some red and some blue paint.

After mixing the once-red pot roughly, he showed his apprentices both pots.

> "Look here, see how they are not well mixed. This red paint has hardly changed its shade. You might think there is less blue paint in this once-red pot than there is red paint in the once-blue pot. But would that be correct?"

Would it?

The Map

Leonardo had been commissioned to create a map of Tuscany for one of his illustrious benefactors. Much of the map was dedicated to drawing the lakes, rivers, and waterways of the region. His map was highly detailed, and geographically accurate.

Upon completion he showed the map to his apprentices, revealing a long river on its way to Rome. He said:

> "You can see here that I have drawn, for the first time, the length of the Tiber river—which we now know to be the third-longest river in Italy. Before I drew this map, which do you think was the third-longest river in Italy?"

The apprentices had a poorer knowledge of geography, and couldn't answer the question he posed.

Can you?

The Important Commission

Leonardo da Vinci was commissioned to create a portrait of the wife of a benefactor. The woman he was asked to paint had a most mysterious beauty, and he welcomed the opportunity to capture some of her enigmatic expression in his work.

In his notebook, he sketched the name of the woman who would sit for him. A somewhat nosy apprentice, wanting to know the subject of his master's latest work, found the sitter's name among several rough sketches—but was dismayed to discover that Leonardo had concealed it in a most intriguing way:

In fact, the young apprentice was unable to decipher the name of the woman at all, despite knowing much of his master's unusual encryptions.

What name had Leonardo written down, according to the sketched inscription above?

The Course of Nature

Leonardo visited a city-state with a watery problem, whereby the river running through it frequently flooded in the spring. This would damage the nearby buildings and bridges.

Privately, he began to devise a scheme to divert the course of the river around the outside walls of the city, thus eliminating the problem of the flooding. He hoped, with a successful plan and a prototype of any necessary machinery, that he might be commissioned by the city's ruler to create the scheme—for a suitable fee, of course.

Firstly, he needed to calculate the volume of water running through the city, both during normal conditions and during the floods. He sent his apprentice out to measure the depth of the river at various points along its banks.

When the flood was due, he sent out the same apprentice with a measuring device that would allow them to keep track of the river's rising levels. It was a rather simple ruler, with notches to mark the high and low points of the river throughout the month. Again, he sent his apprentice out to fix the ruler into place, at the deepest point of the river as he had measured it in the first outing.

The apprentice had originally noted the depth of the river at this point as 2 yards, so he found the point where he had marked "2 yards" and then lowered the ruler into the water until this mark was level with the surface, attaching the device to the side of a floating pontoon which he would be able to access at all times.

Leonardo had calculated that the river would rise by 2 inches every day for a period of 30 days, so had created a long ruler to allow for two yards' rise in the water level in case of exceptional circumstances.

Exactly two weeks after his apprentice had fixed the ruler into place, Leonardo went out to take a reading from his device. What value did the ruler show as the height of the river?

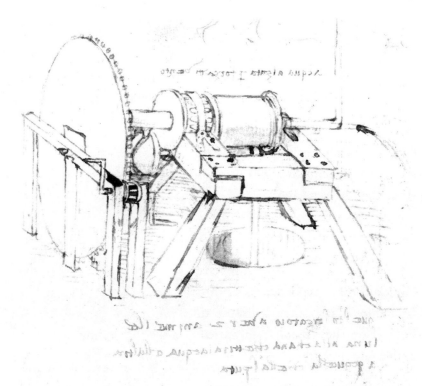

A Man of Many Talents

Leonardo was flicking through a sketchbook to review his recent work. This particular book contained detailed notes on several different subjects, but most notably botany and human anatomy.

On one page he had sketched out a particular flower in very fine detail, next to a body part which he had studied at a dissection.

When he showed the page to an apprentice, the student remarked that the flower and the body part could be captioned with the same four-letter name.

"Indeed," replied Leonardo, "and they both share their name with a Greek goddess."

Which flower and body part were depicted on the page?

Useful Tool

Leonardo was working on the design for a new invention, and asked an apprentice to fetch a tool for him from the workshop.

"What is the tool?" asked the apprentice.

Leonardo replied, "I use it all the time in my writings. It creates an exact copy of anything I use it with and makes two of all my sketches. In fact, it has entirely turned my work around every time I've used it."

What object do you think Leonardo was looking for?

Flying Machines

Leonardo da Vinci had his workshop build three different prototypes of his flying machine, referring to them as "alpha", "beta", and "gamma". Each machine weighed a different amount, and for each machine he tested the glide capabilities, measuring how far it flew when thrown from the roof.

He noted that:

- Beta was heavier than alpha, weighing 4 kg more
- The machine that flew furthest was not the lightest one
- Gamma was the lightest machine, and had two-thirds of the weight of beta
- One glider flew 20 m, which was half as far as the one that went the furthest
- Alpha and beta together weighed a total of 44 kg
- Alpha flew a distance of 30 m

How much did each flying machine weigh, and how far did each one glide?

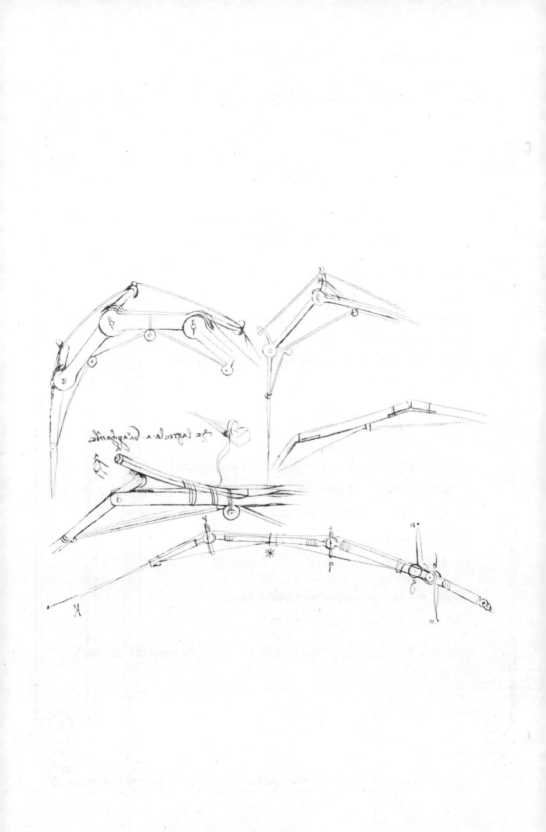

Paint Pigments

Leonardo da Vinci sent one of his apprentices to his store cupboard to collect paint for his latest artwork.

There were three pots of blue paint in the cupboard, each of which had a label and had been made with slightly different amount of pigment. One pot had the label "lapis", another "cobalt", and the third "ultramarine". The three pots were not all equally full, and the three paints had all been mixed at different times.

The apprentice observed that:

- One of the pots was almost full
- The half-full pot had been the first to be mixed
- The ultramarine pot was almost empty
- The lapis pot was not the most recently mixed

Leonardo said, "Bring me the fullest pot—unless another pot has been mixed more recently."

Which pot did the apprentice bring him?

Something
Does Not Add Up

For several months, Leonardo da Vinci had been working on an invention which used mechanical means to calculate numerical totals—that is, a calculator of sorts.

He had created several sketches of the prototype machine, which would function using a series of gear wheels. When he came to build the model, however, the output answers were consistently incorrect. In particular:

- When he entered 2 + 3, the machine gave a solution of 495
- When he entered 3 + 4, the machine gave a solution of 9167
- When he entered 4 + 5, the machine gave a solution of 16259
- When he entered 5 + 6, the machine gave a solution of 253611

Clearly the solutions were wildly incorrect, but at least there was a pattern in the output which could help Leonardo work out what was causing the problem.

What is the pattern? What would the machine give as the solution to 6 + 7?

Fresh Fresco

Two of Leonardo's apprentices were preparing the surface of the wall on the inside of a vast basilica. The wall required careful plastering before it could be painted on: paint was expensive, and why create a masterpiece just to have it ruined by poor, unprepared plasterwork?

The two apprentices worked at different paces, since one was a novice. If the more experienced apprentice had worked alone, it would have taken him twelve hours to prepare the whole wall. Working together, however, it took the two apprentices just eight hours to prepare it.

Assuming that both apprentices work at their own constant rates, how long would it have taken the novice to prepare the wall if they had not been assisted by the more experienced apprentice?

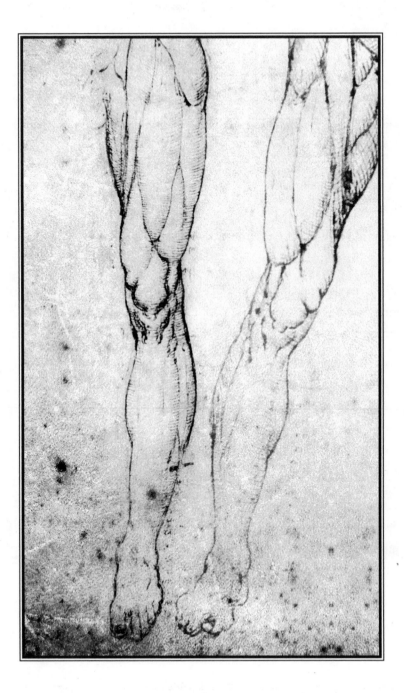

Anatomy Conundrum

Leonardo attended an anatomical dissection performed by a medical professional, and took copious notes during the procedure.

When he returned to the workshop to create sketches based on his notes, however, he found that some had been rendered illegible by rain on the way back. In spite of this, he was still able to discern that:

- The first muscle he was shown was found in the leg
- One of the muscles was the gluteus maximus
- The second muscle shown was found in the chest
- The widest muscles were the latissimus dorsi muscles
- The third muscle he was shown is the body's heaviest
- The sartorius was not the muscle found in the buttocks
- The longest muscle was not the second one shown

He particularly wanted to know which was the longest muscle in the human body, rather than the heaviest or widest. Based on his notes, which is it, and where in the body is it found?

A Series of Events

Leonardo had been working on a design for a building and wanted to include some spiral columns in the architecture. Having made copious mathematical notes, he scribbled down a further note that he felt would be of use to him in the project, and then left his sketchbook open on his worktop.

An apprentice cast his eye over the pages, and in particular the final column sequence that Leonardo was planning to use. In his eagerness to see the design closely, however, he knocked over a bottle of water which—to his despair—quickly flooded the page. Unfortunately, it made one half of the sequence completely unreadable. What remained—the other half—is shown below:

From discarded scraps, the apprentice found the following drafts of the final scribbled note. He decided he would work out which one was correct and re-draw the rest of the sequence back onto the page, hoping Leonardo wouldn't notice.

Which of these four scraps should he use?

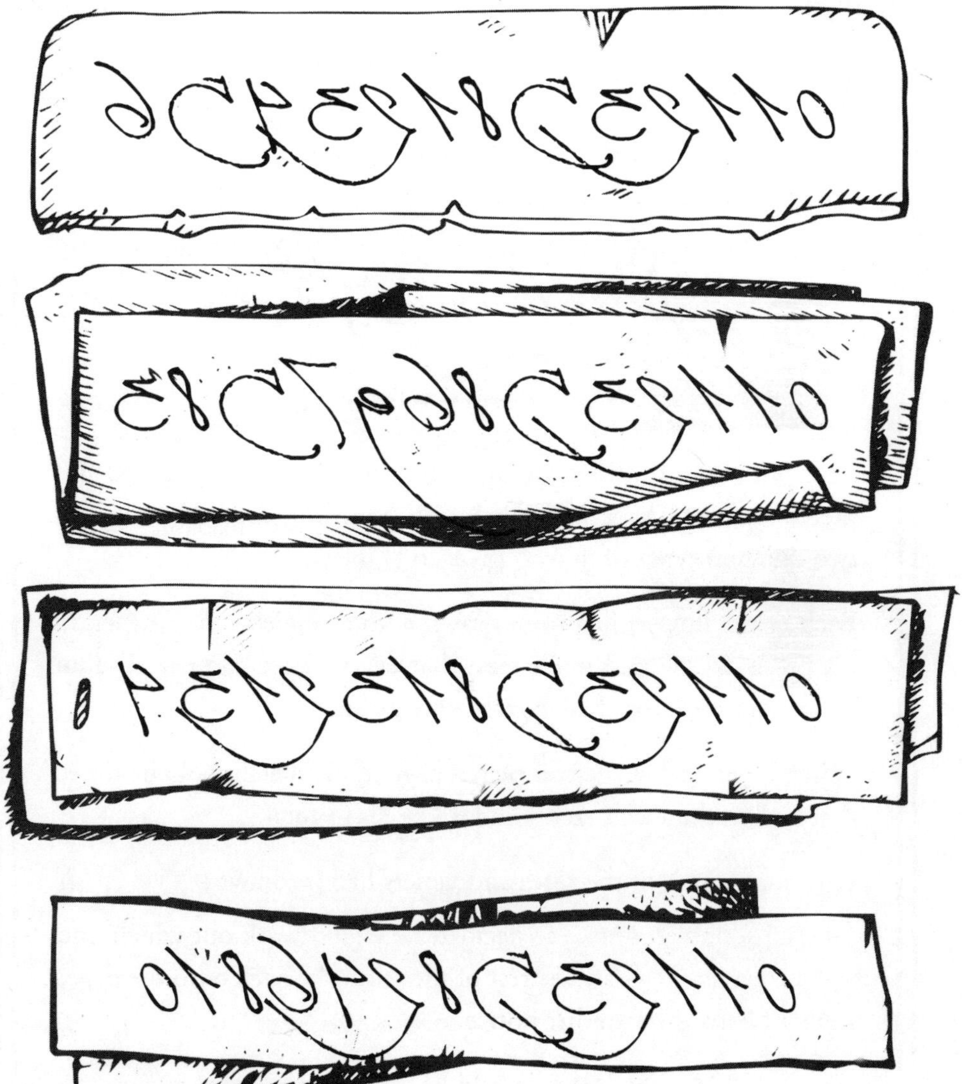

Petals and Stems

Leonardo was putting the finishing touches to a page in his sketchbook which he had filled with beautiful, detailed images of two different types of flower: roses and violets.

Each of the flowers had been drawn with a single stem. Further, in his precision, he had made sure that every violet had exactly four petals and every rose had exactly nine petals.

When he looked at the completed page in his sketchbook, he noted that he had drawn 12 stems and 83 petals in total.

How many each of the roses and violets had he drawn?

A Perfect Sphere

For several months, Leonardo had attempted to create a bronze sculpture of an exact sphere.

When he felt he had finally created a mathematically correct template, he cast a wax prototype and showed it to his apprentices. The resulting model sphere indeed appeared perfect.

He took a piece of chalk and made three small marks on the surface of the wax sculpture. He showed the three marks to his tutees and noted that, without really paying attention to their placement, he had drawn all three marks on the same hemisphere—that is, the same half of the spherical model.

Given the proportions of a perfect sphere, what is the likelihood that the three marks Leonardo drew would all be on the same hemisphere?

A Mountainous Task

Leonardo da Vinci had on multiple occasions climbed the mountain known as Monte Rosa in order to study the play of light, so that he might represent it more accurately in his paintings. From this vantage point he drew sketches of the rest of the Alps and made notes of the weather conditions and their effects on the natural light.

Later, his apprentices found three large sketches and wished to understand the conditions under which he had created them. His jumbled notes allowed them to deduce that:

- The first sketch was made at dusk
- One of the sketches depicted a rainstorm
- The most recent sketch was created with oils
- The sketch made with chalk was not the one drawn at midday
- The sketch made in the morning showed a snowstorm
- The sketch of a hailstorm was made with ink
- The second sketch was made in the morning

In which order did he sketch the storms? At what time of day was each sketch made, and with what material? Remember that Leonardo had climbed the mountain more than once, so the order is not necessarily dawn, midday, and then dusk.

A Handy Tip

Leonardo da Vinci's apprentices were in the workshop copying out some of their master's notes from his copious sketchbooks. Leonardo had the curious habit of encoding his notes in mirrored writing, such that they were both written and read from right to left in many of his writings.

Wanting to make faithful copies, his assistants attempted to mimic their tutor's mirrored writing. Unfortunately, the apprentices kept smudging their freshly inked work and ruining the copied notes while they wrote in this unusual fashion.

Aside from a lack of practice, why might the assistants continuously have smudged their inked notes, but Leonardo seemed to avoid the problem completely? Both he and his assistants were using the same pens and writing materials.

Leonardo's Robot

Leonardo had worked hard to create an automaton for a benefactor, who had dreams of creating a military force of entirely mechanical soldiers.

His latest prototype involved a system of pulleys and cables encased within a metal suit of chain mail. There were three main pulley-cable systems, each controlling a different function of the knight. He had painted the three main cables for ease of reference, and made the following notes for the purpose of testing:

- The three cables are of different lengths
- The red cable causes the automaton to sit
- The shortest cable is yellow
- The green cable is not the one which causes the arms to raise
- The longest cable is not the one which causes the automaton to stand

Before testing, he informed his apprentice that when the mid-length cable of the three was pulled, it also caused the knight's visor to raise.

Which other function did this mid-length cable control, and how had Leonardo painted it?

The Panel Problem

Leonardo da Vinci arrived at the home of a nobleman who had employed him to create a fresco in his palazzo, covering a wall of his ballroom.

To this end, he had drawn out several sketches of a possible mural and had now decided to visit the house to measure the exact proportions of the wall.

When he arrived, however, the wall was not covered in plaster but with wooden panels. Each of the panels had a raised edge, giving the wall the appearance of being covered with empty picture frames.

Leonardo inspected the walls with his benefactor, who proclaimed:

> "The surface is unusual. As you can see, there are two ways you could section out your work: you could paint the three large panels that cross the entire wall, or the eight smaller panels in the middle. Your choice."

But Leonardo could see, in the arrangement of panels, a much greater number of possible rectangular areas once he allowed for those that spanned multiple sections.

How many different rectangles did he observe could be formed, including the one formed by the outer perimeter and all the many smaller possible combinations?

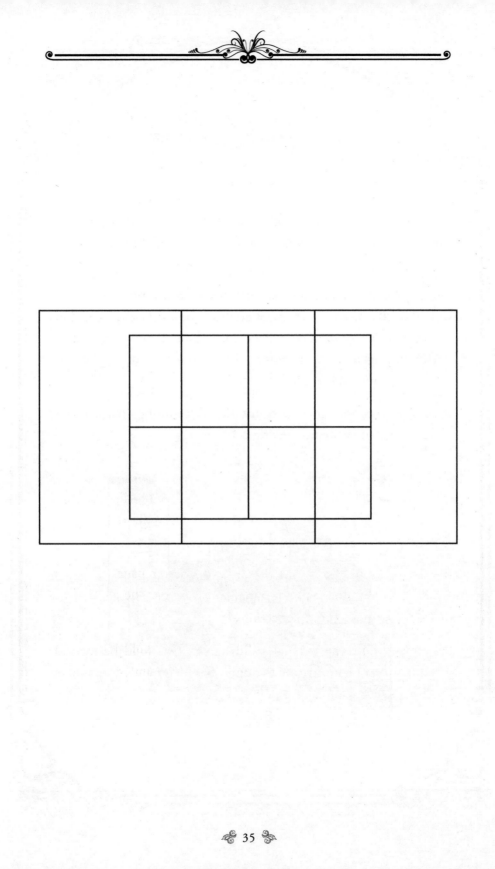

Cubic Question

In order to improve his architectural work Leonardo frequently honed his skill of drawing three-dimensional shapes.

Once he had mastered the art of drafting a single 3D solid, he began to experiment with his sketches. In one such test sketch, he imagined a block consisting of perfect cubes, arranged into a 5 × 4 × 4 formation. He then mentally deducted a number of these cubes and attempted to draw the result, with all the necessary shading and perspective it would require.

How many cubes can you count in the resulting image below? Assume that there are no floating cubes.

Flying Bicycle

After some attempts at designing a flying machine chiefly powered by its pilot's arms, Leonardo turned his attention to other prototypes. Specifically, he began to work on a device which would make use of a rider's leg muscles to power the machine. He drew up sketches for what would become known as a "flying bicycle".

When it came to building the prototypes, Leonardo struggled with the stability of the machine, and decided to add an additional wheel and extra gears. After more testing, however, the machine still would not work successfully.

As a general point of logic, why do you think that he was unable to build a three-wheeled flying bicycle?

Perfect Match

Leonardo had spent his day studying the Platonic solids, and in particular the icosahedron—a solid structure consisting of 20 faces, each face in the shape of an equilateral triangle. Before attempting to sketch the icosahedron in three dimensions, however, he wanted to build a model of it to study.

He gathered a pile of matchsticks and cut them to exactly equal sizes. He laid out three of them and fixed them together at their ends, so that they created a triangle shape.

This triangle could be a single face of the icosahedron, and in such a shape each single matchstick would therefore form one edge of a face of the icosahedron.

What is the smallest number of matchsticks Leonardo would need to build his three-dimensional model of the icosahedron, given that such a solid would be made of 20 identical faces like the one shown on the page opposite?

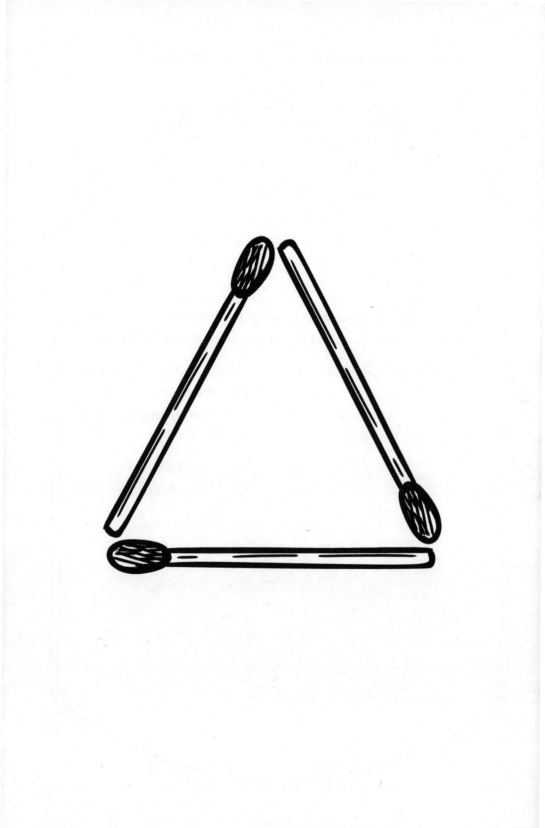

Caught in the Net

Continuing his study of the Platonic solids, Leonardo began to work out how he might accurately draw an octahedron. This structure would have eight faces, with each face once again in the shape of an equilateral triangle.

To this end, he decided to construct a version of this three-dimensional shape made of card, so that he might study it better.

He began by drawing several drafts of a shape net that he could use to create the model octahedron. But which of the four options here is the only net which could actually be cut out and folded along the lines to make an octahedron without any missing faces?

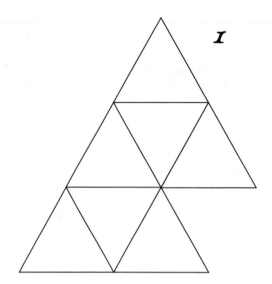

I

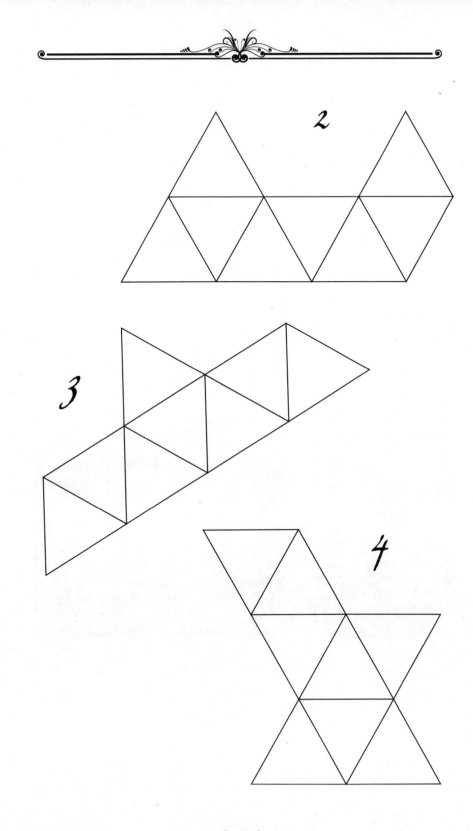

All at Sea

Leonardo had been working on an idea for a new marine vessel. He kept his various plans and notes relating to the project a complete secret, however, since he thought his new invention might become useful in naval warfare and he wished to prevent his plans from falling into enemy hands.

In total, he built five different prototypes for his new watercraft.

One day he took all five models out to a waterway in the city, in order to test them. Four of the small ships floated on the water's surface, but one of them sank beneath it.

Once he had returned to the workshop, Leonardo broke up the four models that had remained afloat, but began to make improvements to the one that sank.

Why might he want to work further on the vessel which sank, rather than the four which did not?

A Dicey Game 1

In his workshop, Leonardo da Vinci was busy rolling and re-rolling a regular six-sided dice. He planned to make notes on the results of his throws, so that he might compare the real outcomes against the predictions he made beforehand.

According to his initial predictions, he felt that if he rolled the dice six times, the most likely result would be that each number on the dice would be produced exactly once.

By the end of his first experiment, the following had occurred:

- His first roll produced an odd number
- The second roll also produced an odd number
- The third roll produced a number which was the sum of the first two numbers
- The fourth roll produced a number which was the sum of the first and third numbers
- The fifth roll produced a number which was the product of the second and sixth numbers
- The sixth roll produced an even number

After six rolls of the dice, Leonardo saw that his prediction was correct. Therefore, what numbers did he throw on each roll of the 6-sided dice?

Number Sets 1

In his notebook, Leonardo wrote out the digits from 1 to 9, and then organized them into three sets as follows:

Set 1

4   6   8

Set 2

2   3   5   7

Set 3

9

What rule had he used to organize the numbers into their sets?

Unfriendly Fire

Leonardo da Vinci created a prototype of a military gunboat to show off to potential investors. Designed in the shape of a circle, the boat was built to carry 20 cannons, each spaced out equally around the circular circumference of the boat.

Each of the cannons faced outward from the middle of the ship, with their fuse-lighting ends in the middle of the deck. The cannons were arranged so that someone carrying a flame could light them all rapidly, creating a weapon which could fire in all directions within a very short space of time, even if manned by just a single person.

In fact, whoever lit the fuses would have so short a distance to walk between cannons that there would be only one second's delay between lighting one fuse and the next.

Given this timing, how long would it take a single person to light all 20 fuses on the ship?

Future Improvements

In his studio, Leonardo was working on a new design. It was not a new invention, but rather he was making improvements to a machine which already existed. He felt that current models of this particular instrument were not sufficiently accurate to be fit for his purposes.

After he had created a new mechanism for the inner workings of the device, Leonardo carried out a test of the machine, during which he made the following notes:

- Adding 4 to 9 gives 1
- Adding 9 to 7 gives 4
- Adding 7 to 6 gives 1

Leonardo was therefore satisfied that his new design worked perfectly.

What device had he been trying to improve?

Family Values

Leonardo was commissioned by a patron to create a family portrait of that selfsame patron and his immediate family.

Before accepting the commission, however, he wanted to confirm how many figures would need to be included in the painting, as the patron and his wife had several children.

Said the patron:

> "Well, each of my daughters has as many brothers as they do sisters, but each of my sons has twice as many sisters as they do brothers—if that helps."

Leonardo said that it did, and began to calculate the paint that he would need to complete the painting.

How many children did the patron have?

How Many Hulls?

Leonardo had been working on a design for a multi-hulled boat, thinking that seafaring merchants might benefit from the extra stability that additional hulls would lend during long voyages.

He built three prototypes to test his theory: a standard boat with one hull, a boat with two hulls, and a boat with three hulls. He gave them each a different name, and loaded each of them with a different cargo for testing.

He took these small models down to a nearby lake, and measured how far each model sailed with a single push from the water's edge, with no wind. None of the boats sank.

- The boat that made it the shortest distance was loaded with a pile of books
- The boat he had named *Iota* did not travel a square number of yards
- *Zeta* made a distance of three yards
- The boat carrying paintbrushes had three hulls
- The boat named *Delta* covered two-thirds of the distance that *Iota* did
- The boat stacked up with shoes journeyed for six yards
- The books were placed on a single-hulled boat

At the water's edge, Leonardo was approached by a merchant who was interested in his creations. The merchant asked about the boat that had two hulls. What was its name, and how far did it travel?

Code Conundrum

Leonardo had had built, according to his detailed plans, a wooden box which could be mechanically locked via a series of hidden inner gears. The gears—and therefore the wooden box—could be unlocked with a five-digit code, which he had chosen himself.

Leonardo wrote some cryptic notes in his sketchbook that revealed the code, without directly divulging the five-digit number that was needed.

His notes were as follows:

- The five digits sum to 18
- The digit values increase in both directions from the central digit of the code reading outward
- The code can be mirrored left to right, or read upside down, and still appear the same

What was the code to the box?

Proportional Representation

Leonardo had been studying the human form and, in particular, the relative proportions of the body parts to a person's height.

He had closely studied the measurements of one of his apprentices to make his calculations, and wrote down the following notes:

- Arm span (fingertip to fingertip) = total height
- Top of head to chin = one eighth of total height
- Total shoulder width = one quarter of total height
- Foot length = one seventh of total height
- Elbow to fingertip = one quarter of total height

Leonardo used a ruler to measure the distance from the apprentice's left elbow to the edge of his left shoulder, which resulted in a measurement of 21 cm.

Assuming that the model had no missing limbs and had the proportions as given in Leonardo's notes, what was the height of the man—and what was the length of one of his feet?

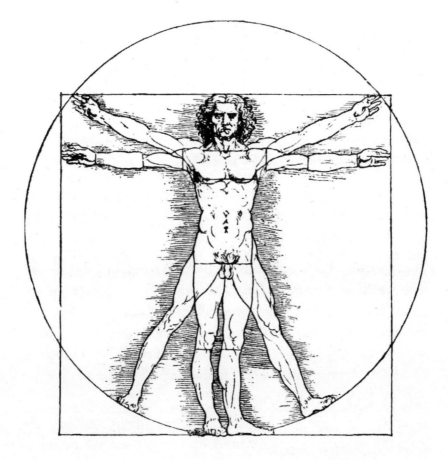

The Water Test

Leonardo da Vinci was putting the finishing touches to a design for a steam-powered engine, and was ready to find out if it worked.

He needed exactly five gallons of water in order to test his machine, and sent one of his apprentices out to the canal to obtain the necessary amount of water.

The apprentice, however, could only find two vessels in the workshop with which to measure and carry the water to Leonardo from the canal. The first held exactly three gallons of liquid when full, and the second held exactly seven gallons of water when full. Neither of them had any other measurements inscribed, so the apprentice could not use them to accurately measure smaller quantities.

How could the apprentice use just those two vessels to measure out five gallons of water for his mentor, without estimating or using any other measuring equipment?

Structural Query

After spending some time in the airy palazzo of his Milanese benefactor, Leonardo decided to draw up some designs for a new workshop. He wished to design a central uncovered courtyard where he could study natural light, and a long gallery to store his works in progress.

The inner courtyard would be a perfect square, with its area exactly matching the area of the long rectangular gallery leading up to it. The gallery would measure exactly nine yards in length, and the comparatively narrower width of the gallery would be two-thirds of the width of the inner courtyard.

If the walls of the inner courtyard were designed to be a whole number of yards in length (i.e. an exact number of yards without any fractional amount), then what would be the area of each of the spaces, and what would be the width of the gallery?

Sleep Cycle

Leonardo's apprentices noticed that he had adopted an unusual sleeping pattern since he had begun work on a large mural inside the city's basilica. Specifically, they noticed that he slept for exactly 20 minutes in every four-hour period.

This particular commission took the artist precisely one calendar month to complete, beginning at midnight on the first day of the month and finishing at midnight on the last day of the month (when measured using the modern calendar). Leonardo both started and finished his work on the same day of the week.

How many hours did Leonardo sleep for in total, while he worked on the project?

The Ideal City

Frustrated with the lack of infrastructure in the place he inhabited, Leonardo set about designing an ideal city. It would be built around a series of waterways which could power mills, facilitate transport, control irrigation, and flush the sewers. Once he had designed the structure of the various canals and waterways, he began to add buildings to his plans.

On the first day, Leonardo drew two buildings on his plan. On the second, he drew the same amount as the first day plus an extra one, and then on the third day he drew in the same number as the second day plus an extra two.

His apprentice suspected that Leonardo would draw eight buildings on the fourth day: the same number as the previous day plus an extra three. In fact, Leonardo drew one fewer building than his apprentice estimated, and on the fifth day he drew twice the number of buildings he had drawn on the third day plus an extra one.

The apprentice remarked to Leonardo that his sequence was uncharacteristically unpredictable. His master, however, denied this—he claimed that the pattern was easily predictable.

What was the pattern, and if he continued to follow it, then how many buildings do you think he drew on the sixth day?

Planning Problem

While creating his designs for an ideal city, Leonardo took a walk along the main road in the real city he lived in, to measure the distance to the main square from the city gate. He took an apprentice with him to keep notes, although the road was completely straight and would have been straightforward to measure. Before he began, he had calculated that his stride was exactly one yard in length.

After taking 140 strides from the city gate—covering a distance of 140 yards toward the main square—the apprentice realized he had dropped his pencil somewhere along the route, and was unable to take down the measurements he needed.

Both he and Leonardo went back on themselves along the straight road to find the pencil, but they did not keep count of the number of strides they took to reach it—and therefore how far they had returned toward the city gate. They retrieved the pencil and continued toward the main square in the same way as before. Leonardo took 160 strides after their hiatus, so the square was 160 yards from the point at which the pencil was retrieved.

At the main square, the apprentice exclaimed that their measurements so far were useless, and they would have to start the count again, this time walking from the main square back toward the city gate. They did so, and noted down the total number of strides Leonardo took along the straight road back to the gate on this second, uninterrupted walk.

How far did Leonardo walk in total, from when he first left the city gate until he returned back to it, including his detour to retrieve the dropped pencil?

The Uncommon Clock

Leonardo's assistant was walking through the marketplace in a new city, and looked up at the clock in the main square. His vision was fading from many hours of staring at objects right in front of him, but he could make out that the hour hand pointed to what looked like a "1". He knew from this that he was on time for his meeting, and was pleased.

After his meeting, however, he crossed back over the main square and looked up at the clock, where he was shocked to see that the hour hand was now pointing to what looked very much like "11".

The assistant estimated, however, that only an or so had passed since he last looked at the clock.

Can you explain this discrepancy in the apparent times?

The Hidden Agenda

One of Leonardo da Vinci's apprentices was in charge of the virtuosic maestro's agenda, whereby his job was to keep track of important dates.

When a potential patron came by the workshop to ask about the painter's availability for a project, Leonardo spoke to the apprentice in charge of the diary:

> "This morning I wrote down my availability for the week in my agenda. What two days did I write down as being available?"

Leonardo had written down two consecutive days in the agenda, although when translated into modern English, none of them was Tuesday or Thursday, or a weekend.

Which two days had he written in?

No Neutral Tones

Leonardo had been working on a project with a friend, and it was now almost complete. They had each created a set of small sculptures, where each man's set was exactly the same as the other man's, apart from the fact that each had chosen stone of a particular hue with which to sculpt all of their models.

Within each man's set, several of the pieces had been duplicated: three different sculptures had each been created with an identical twin, and one sculpture had been replicated eight times. Each set also had two figures that were made only once each.

What had the two friends been sculpting?

The Coin Conundrum

At his workbench, Leonardo da Vinci was checking the payment given to him by a local benefactor, which he saw amounted to five silver coins and one gold one. All six coins were exactly the same size.

When he laid the coins out flat on his bench, Leonardo felt that the payment of an additional silver coin would have been appreciated, not least so that he could complete the pattern in which he had arranged the coins, with the gold coin in the middle:

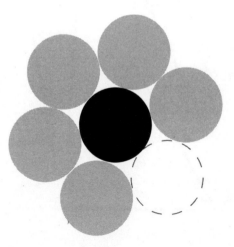

Without needing a seventh coin to complete the arrangement, how could he now rearrange these six coins that he *did* have so that every silver coin was touching two other silver coins, and yet the gold coin still touched every silver coin?

Paintbrush Positions

After another afternoon spent studying the mathematical properties of triangles and other geometric shapes, Leonardo decided to test the mental prowess of his students.

On his desk lay six paintbrush handles, each exactly the same length. He picked up three of them and arranged them into an equilateral triangle, like this:

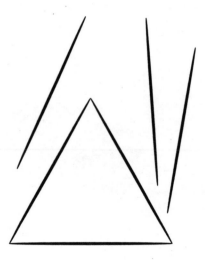

He then set his students a challenge: how they could arrange these six handles so that they formed exactly four identical equilateral triangles? Furthermore, the arrangement must be done without the paintbrush handles touching one another—except at a point, as in the triangle he had already made.

How can it be done?

Pigment Problem

Leonardo da Vinci had ordered a pot of expensive blue pigment for use on a religious mural. The pigment—identified by the label "ultramarine"—needed to be mixed with water before it could be applied.

Given the value of the pigment, it was important that the paint was mixed to the right proportions, so that it was neither too thick nor too thin.

When the pigment arrived, Leonardo mixed up exactly one pint of paint, consisting of 99 percent water. The mixture turned out to be too thin, however, so he asked an apprentice to leave it outside in the sun so that some of the water would evaporate. The apprentice later brought the paint back into the workshop when it was 98 percent water.

What volume of paint did Leonardo now have in the container? Assume that no pigment has evaporated.

Instrumental Notes

In his notebook, Leonardo da Vinci wrote out the names of several local musicians for whom he wanted to create personalized musical instruments.

He wrote down the names of these musicians in a specific order:

1. Domenico

2. Renato

3. Michelangelo

4. Fabrizio

5. Sofia

6. Laura

7. Silvio

Why do you think he wrote the names in this particular order, and which name was therefore the odd one out?

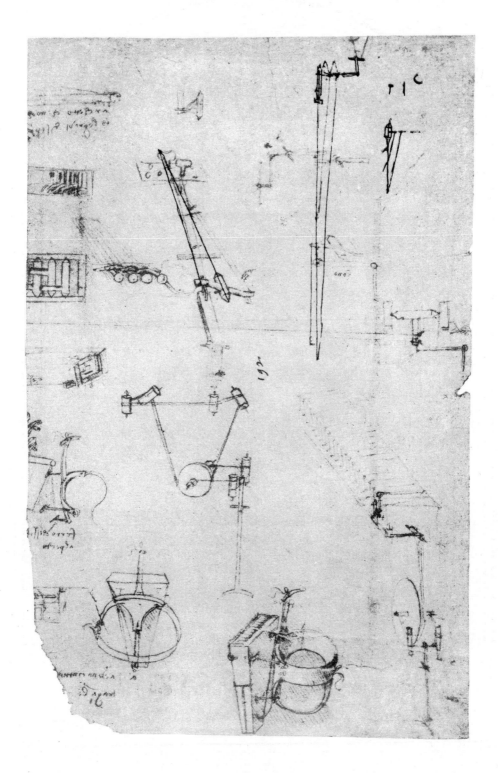

The Moon and its Moods

Leonardo had been taking note of the phases of the moon in an attempt to account for irregularities in its brilliance. Each night for a month, he climbed onto the roof of a different nearby building and recorded the brightness of the moon as best as he could.

At the end of the month he looked back at his notes, which covered his three most significant recordings:

- The recording of the full moon was made at midnight
- The recording made at 2 am showed the moon as half-full
- The recording of the new moon was not the one made from the roof of the university
- The recording made at 10 pm was made from the roof of the basilica
- The full moon was not the phase recorded from the roof of the workshop

From which location did Leonardo record the full moon?

The Pay Rise

Leonardo had received a second payment from a particular patron, which this time consisted of nine silver coins.

After a day studying the internal angles of geometric shapes, Leonardo amused himself in the evening as he laid out the coins in the shape of a right-angled triangle:

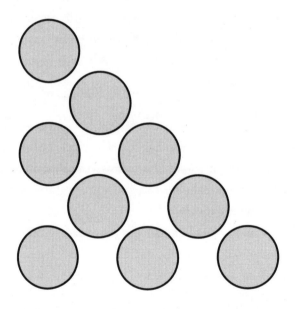

He then proceeded to rearrange the coins into a square formation. What is the minimum number of coins he needed to touch in order to achieve this?

The Arm Spans

As part of his studies of human proportion—and in preparation for creating a flying machine—Leonardo da Vinci measured the arm span of each of the students currently present in his workshop.

- All of the arm spans were between 120 cm and 200 cm
- The final two digits in the first measurement taken were the reverse of the final two digits in the third measurement taken
- Franco's arm span was measured first, and was found to be 1 cm greater than Giulio's
- Cosimo's arm span was measured immediately after the span that was a cube number
- The second digit in Giulio's measurement was one greater than the first digit, and the third digit was one greater than the second digit
- Matteo's arm span was measured immediately before Pietro's
- The final measurement was the greatest taken, and a square number with repeated digits

In what order did the apprentices have their measurements taken, and what were they?

Masterpiece Mix-Up

While looking through the accounts for the workshop, one of Leonardo's apprentices noticed that his tutor had still not been paid for a painting he'd created some years ago. It was the most recent of five finished portraits for which Leonardo had used real-life models.

From the accounts, the apprentice saw the following notes:

- *Lady with an Ermine* was created earlier than *La Belle Ferronnière*
- *Portrait of a Musician* was created immediately following *Ginevra de' Benci*
- *La Belle Ferronnière* was created earlier than *La Gioconda*
- *Portrait of a Musician* was created earlier than *Lady with an Ermine*

Which painting had Leonardo not been paid for?

Time and Time Again

Leonardo's newest apprentice was attempting to build a clock according to plans drawn up by his tutor. He asked for the current time, planning to set the clock at that time and then come back to it later to see if it had worked accurately.

His master gave the following answer:

> "Ask me in three hours. Then it will be twice as long until noon as it would be if you were to ask me ninety minutes after the time in three hours."

What time was it now?

Benevolent Benefactors

Leonardo had received a large commission for a portrait from a friend and nobleman, who had in return promised the artist a complete new set of brushes to accompany his already significant fee.

In an attempt to clear out his workshop, Leonardo decided to gift his current five apprentices the old set of brushes, to be shared out among themselves in whatever way they pleased for their personal use.

- Giacomo was the first to choose; he took half of the available brushes, plus an extra two
- Ambrogio chose next, and took a quarter of the remaining brushes, plus an extra one
- Bernardino was the next to choose, and took five brushes from the pile that remained
- Cesare chose fourth, and took a third of the remaining brushes, plus an extra one
- Martino then took all five of the brushes that were left

How many brushes had Leonardo had in the first place, and how many did each apprentice take?

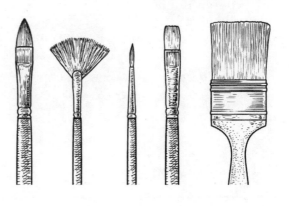

The Bonus

After completing a particularly complicated commission, Leonardo da Vinci decided to give his apprentices a small pecuniary bonus in recognition of their hard work.

He had placed six silver coins into a pouch—one coin for each of the six apprentices in his workshop.

When all six apprentices had received their silver coins, however, there was still one coin left in the pouch.

Leonardo had not miscalculated, so how could this situation arise?

A Loaded Question

In order to be able to begin work on a commissioned sculpture, Leonardo da Vinci needed to order two perfectly cuboid blocks of marble for his studio. His plan was to try his design out on a smaller block, and then create his final work on a larger one.

Leonardo asked his apprentice to place an order for two blocks, specifying that they must be made of exactly the same marble, and that one block should be exactly four times as heavy as the other.

The apprentice ordered the blocks, making sure that the length, width, and heights of one of the blocks were exactly four times the respective length, width, and heights of the smaller block.

Had the apprentice calculated correctly? Or, if not, how many times heavier would the larger block be than the smaller one?

Rescue Mission

Leonardo da Vinci was testing out a prototype of an ironclad boat on a small, circular lake. The prototype had worked well, but the device had broken down in the middle of the lake, with no sail on its mast and therefore no wind acting to bring it back to the shore. Nor was there any current that could do so.

The boat was 20 yards from the shore, and although it was too far out for either Leonardo or the apprentice he had taken with him to reach, they did have a rope with them.

How could the two men use the rope to retrieve the boat, without entering the water themselves or relying on the luck of somehow throwing the rope into the middle of the lake and lassoing the boat?

It might be helpful to know that the rope was 40 yards long.

Fetch and Carry

Two of Leonardo da Vinci's apprentices were preparing to deliver a finished masterpiece to its new home, and bring back the silver ingots that had been promised as payment.

Giacomo carried the painting for the first 15 miles toward its new owner's house, and then Silvio carried it for the rest of the journey.

The two then journeyed back along the same route. Giacomo carried the heavy bag of silver ingots for the first part of the journey, then gave it to Silvio to carry for the final stretch of the journey—at the point of this handover they still had 10 miles still to travel.

Assuming the two apprentices only carried the painting and the ingots as described above, and no further, then which of them had walked the furthest in total while carrying the painting and then the ingots? For how many miles further had they carried them?

The Military Model

Leonardo had sketched out various designs for a military weapon which could have several small cannons mounted onto it, all able to be fired almost simultaneously.

Based on his sketches, he designed two model prototypes. The two structures each had capacity for a differing number of cannons. In fact, to be precise, one could hold 50 percent more cannons than the other.

To test out the functionality of the designs, Leonardo had his apprentices build several model cannons to mount onto the two structures.

There were enough cannons to fill all the mounts on one of the models, with an additional four cannons left over. The other model, however, had more mounts than there were cannons—and when all of the cannons built by the workshop had been loaded on, there was still space for eight more.

How many cannons had Leonardo's apprentices built?

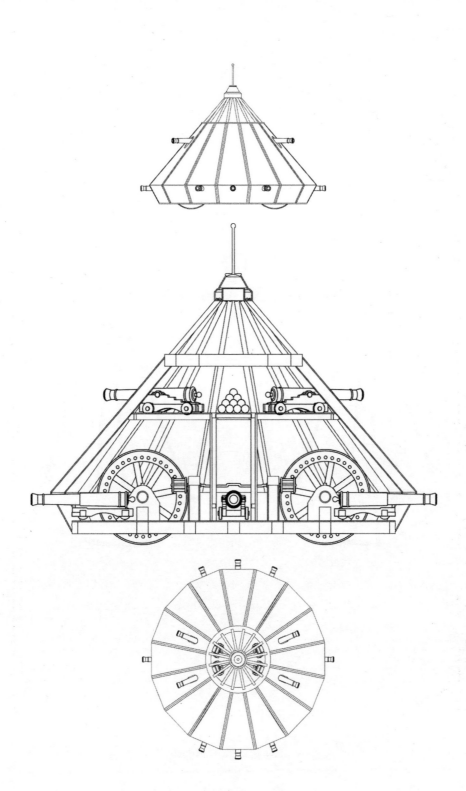

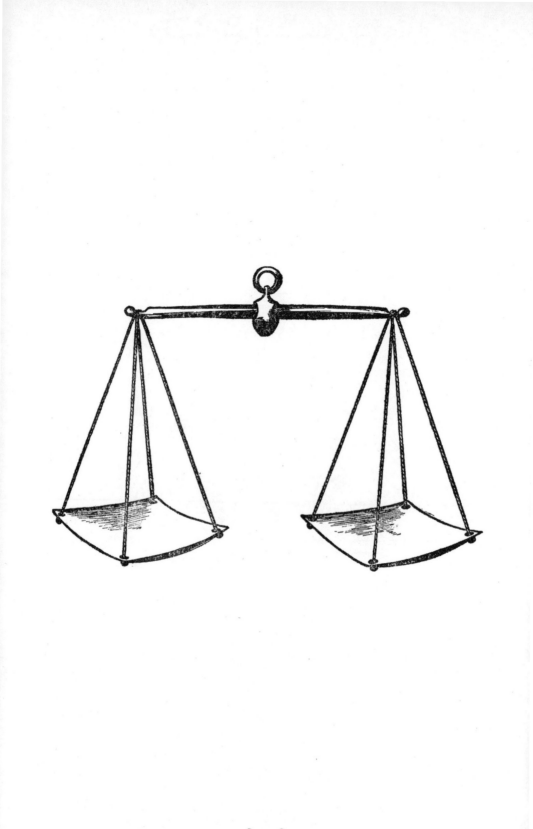

Weighty Decisions

Keen to improve on contemporary technology, Leonardo da Vinci had created a prototype for a self-indicating weighing scale to replace his balancing scales. The balancing scales required a separate set of weights to be able to function, so a device which could reveal an object's weight with no further assistance would be considerably quicker to use.

To test his new prototype, he set it up next to a set of traditional balancing scales. He had seven coins with which he planned to test his device: four bronze, two silver, and one gold.

He noted first that his balancing scale was perfectly balanced when exactly one of each type of coin was placed on one side of the scale, and all of the remaining coins on the other side.

If he now removed a single bronze coin and placed it on his self-indicating scales, what weight should it show the single bronze coin as having?

Assume that each coin of the same type weighed exactly the same as other coins of that type, and that Leonardo knew in advance that the gold coin weighed exactly 84 g.

The Test of Time

Leonardo was completing model prototypes for a spring-loaded clock.

He wanted to test his model against two other timepieces which he knew to be reliable.

One of the timepieces had no moving parts at all, whereas the other timepiece had thousands.

Which two devices did he want to test his clock against?

Clay figures

Leonardo had been studying human anatomy and creating small sculptures of anatomically correct figures, to help him with his myriad sketches and paintings.

In his workshop, he created each of his sculptures from blocks of clay which were all identical in size. Each figure was sculpted from a single one of these clay blocks, although for every three sculptures made, there was enough clay left over to create one more block.

How many blocks would Leonardo have needed to order, so that he had enough clay to make 54 sculptures?

The Scale of Things 1

Leonardo da Vinci had created an aerial map of the city he lived in for a benefactor, who hoped to use it for strategic military purposes. The map was remarkably accurate and had been based on several sketches of map fragments that Leonardo had made while walking around the city on foot.

One of the sketches, on which the final map was based, had been drawn at two-thirds of the scale of the final map. The final map, in turn, had been drawn at a scale of 1:10,000.

If the road from the city gate to the main square was drawn at a length of 18 cm on the sketch, how long was the road in real life? Assume that the sketch and the final map were equally accurate.

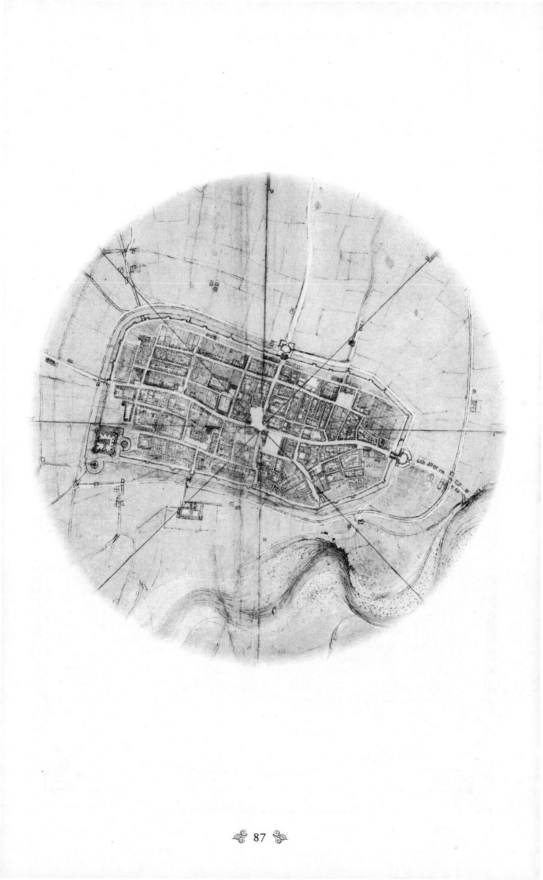

The Throwaway Design

Leonardo had been working hard on a new design in his workshop.

After several failed attempts to create a successful prototype, he threw his latest designs from the roof of the workshop. They all fell straight down toward the ground.

After throwing them from the roof, however, Leonardo realized that one of his most recent designs had been a success.

What had he been designing?

Shades of Shades

In his studio, Leonardo da Vinci was conducting an experiment on the mixing of different pigments.

He lined up several small, empty glass vials next to one another, then added the same volume of umber pigment into each vial.

Next, he added one drop of water to the first vial, two drops of water to the second, three to the third, and so on. He then mixed the contents within each vial to create a paint solution, with each vial creating a different shade of umber that became lighter in tone as the number of added water drops increased.

Overall, he had added 153 drops of water to the vials.

How many different shades had he created?

Watching the Clock

Leonardo da Vinci had been working on a plan for a spring-loaded clock, with the hope that it could operate without requiring a series of pendulums to keep the pieces in motion.

Once he had designed a prototype, he had some of his apprentices build a model according to his careful plans.

He then began a test. Starting at 12:15 pm, he ensured the clock was set accordingly. Two hours later, however, the clock showed a time of 3:10 pm. Then, after a further two hours, the time shown was 3:20 pm.

Assuming that his design was correct, what simple mistake could the apprentices have made when assembling the clock?

The Supper Sketches

In preparation for painting *The Last Supper*, Leonardo da Vinci sketched out in his notebook the figures who would appear in the final fresco. Several of the figures were sketched multiple times, as he tried to determine the position in which each person should be painted.

After the great work had been completed, Leonardo returned to his sketchbook and made the following observations:

- He had drawn three-quarters of the number of sketches of John as he did of Peter
- There were three times as many sketches of Judas as of John
- In total, he had drawn 48 sketches of these three men

How many sketches of Judas were there?

The Scale of Things 2

When Leonardo was finalizing his city map, he placed one of his sketches on top of the final map at the same orientation.

The sketch was more or less identical to the larger map, but was around a third of its size. The outer borders of the smaller sketch were completely contained within the outer borders of the final map.

Looking at the two charts, he realized that the location of the basilica on the smaller sketch was precisely on top of the basilica he had drawn on the larger map.

What is the likelihood that one of the locations on the smaller sketch would have been placed exactly on top of the same feature on the larger map?

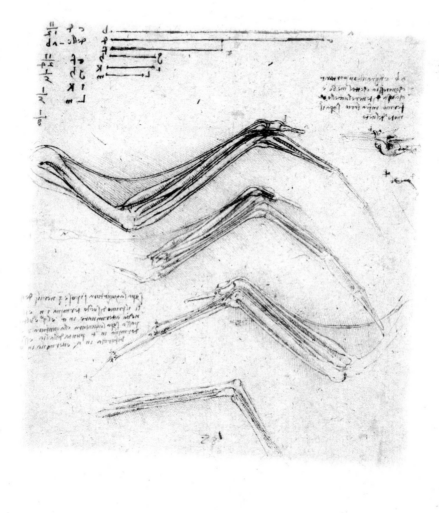

The Wingspans

During the creation of the plans for one of his flying machines, Leonardo da Vinci drew careful anatomical sketches of the wings of several birds. Indeed, on just one single page of his notebook, he had drawn five birds of different sizes and annotated them with the width of their wingspans.

He later asked an apprentice to label each of the birds with their names, but the tutee could not tell which bird was which by sight. When the apprentice asked Leonardo which bird was which, Leonardo gave the following reply:

> "The eagle had the largest wingspan, which was five times larger than that of the sparrow, whereas the lark's wingspan was only 50 percent larger than the sparrow's.

> "The kite's wingspan was twice that of the lark's, and the difference between the wingspan of the thrush and the lark was a quarter of the sparrow's total wingspan, with the lark's wingspan being smaller than the thrush's."

If the smallest wingspan of the five birds was 20 cm, what were all of the other birds' wingspans?

Taking Stock

Leonardo was looking around his workshop and counting the number of unfinished canvases leaning up against the walls.

- Some of the canvases featured only pencil sketches
- He noticed that there were five times as many canvases with only water-based paint as there were those with just pencil
- He also observed that there were twice as many with just oil paint applied as just pencil
- Additionally, three of the canvases had chalk drawings on them

If only one type of art material had been used on each canvas, and only these four types of art material had been used on the 35 unfinished canvases in the workshop, then how many of them had had oil paint applied?

Inky Issues

Due to a supply problem, Leonardo da Vinci needed to ration the amount of ink he was using to make the copious notes in his workbooks.

At the start of the first week of the year, there were 55 full pots of ink in the workshop. That week, Leonardo used a certain number of those pots in their entirety.

On each subsequent week until his next delivery, he used one fewer pot than he had used the preceding week, but always using the pots in their entirety.

Eventually the week arrived when he only had one pot of ink left to last the whole week.

Including the week with just a single pot left, how many weeks had his supply of ink lasted for?

Solar Solution

Leonardo had been working on putting together plans for a machine that could use the sun's energy to function—that is, a solar-powered device. In particular, he was interested in using the sun's rays to create a hot water supply in Florence.

His patron reviewed the designs and noted that they were certainly ingenious, and observed that he had never seen anything like them before.

Leonardo noted, however, that the patron had surely come across at least one device which needed the sun's rays to function. Moreover, it had been invented well over a thousand years previously.

What device was Leonardo speaking of, which might have been displayed outside the patron's own house?

Walking on Water 2

Leonardo decided it was time to test the device he had created to allow a wearer to walk on water.

It was determined that an apprentice should wear the water-walking device and try to stay afloat on a nearby decorative lake, which was perfectly circular, for as long as possible.

The middle of the lake was 45 yards from the shore, and the apprentice managed to walk all the way to the midpoint in a straight line, and at a constant pace, before he unfortunately started to sink. He then swam back from the middle at a speed which was a third of his water-walking speed.

If the return swim had taken the apprentice one and a half minutes to complete at a constant pace, then how long would it have taken him to cross the whole lake using the water-walking device if he had not sunk?

Turn the Time

Leonardo da Vinci wanted to test the capacity of a steam-powered device he had been working on, and so set it up next to three hourglasses which each took different amounts of time for all of their sand to pass through them.

The first hourglass measured a period of 2 minutes, the second measured 5 minutes, and the third measured 7 minutes.

Leonardo wanted to use the hourglasses to measure out exactly 10 minutes of time, so he could run the steam-powered device for

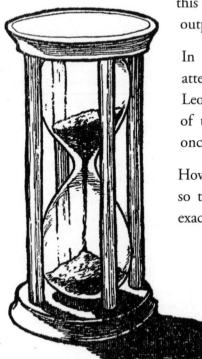

this fixed period and then measure its output.

In order to be able to fully pay attention to the steam device, Leonardo did not want to turn any of the hourglasses over more than once each.

How could he use the hourglasses so that together they measured out exactly 10 minutes of time?

A Perfect Circle

In order to prepare for his great sketch of *The Vitruvian Man*, Leonardo had been sketching a variety of circles. It was difficult to draw a perfect circle with no additional tools, but he felt it was a skill he needed to hone.

After making several attempts, Leonardo was satisfied that he had finally drawn a single, perfect circle. Can you spot it among the rest of his drafts below?

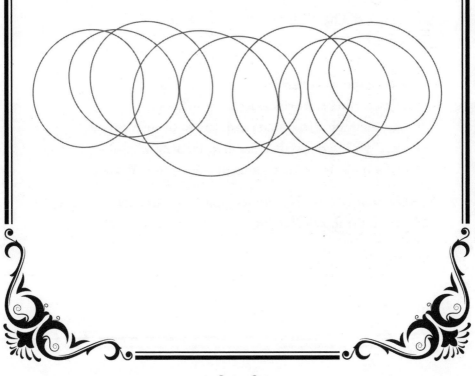

Apprentice Appraisal

One day, Leonardo was holding interviews for a new apprentice to join his workshop.

He spoke to each potential candidate and inspected their portfolios during a series of individual meetings.

At the end of the day, Leonardo looked back at the notes he had made in his notebook, using them to help him decide on the best candidate for the job. Unfortunately, however, he had not written down the names of the apprentices he had seen during each meeting, although he did have a list of all of their names.

After a minute's reflection, he recalled the following points:

- Alessandro was interviewed later than Francesco
- Luca was interviewed earlier than Stefano
- Giovanni was the second candidate to be interviewed
- Luca was interviewed earlier than Francesco
- Stefano was interviewed immediately before Alessandro

He then realized that he definitely wanted to hire the candidate he had seen in the fourth meeting.

Who was it?

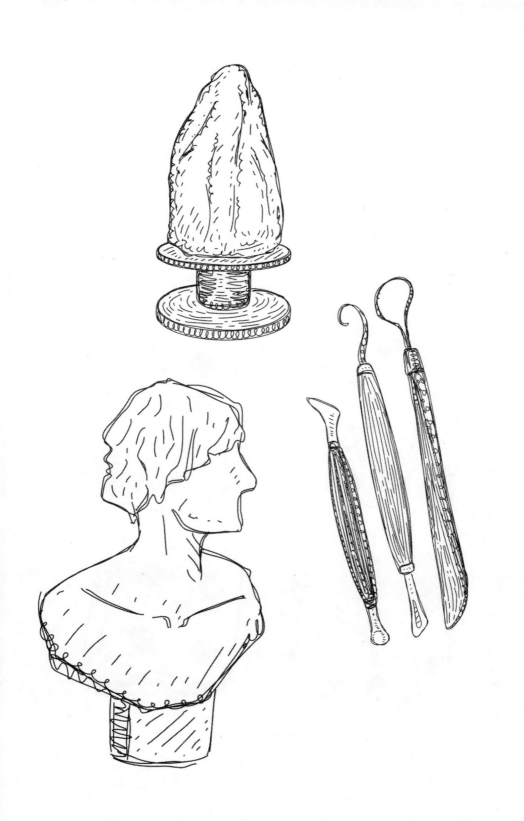

A Dicey Game 2

In his workshop, Leonardo was rolling a regular six-sided dice. He was making notes on the results of his throws, and how frequently his predictions turned out to be correct, so that he might compare these outcomes against the chances he had calculated in advance.

His prediction was that, if he rolled the dice six times, each number on the dice would alternate between even and odd with each successive throw.

After the end of the six experimental rolls, he made the following notes:

- The first three numbers rolled were in line with his prediction
- The number shown on the first roll was three times the value of the one shown on the third roll
- The product of the third and fifth rolls was equal to the number shown on the first roll
- The number rolled second was not the smallest
- Each possible number was rolled exactly once
- The sum of the second and fourth rolls was equal to the number shown on the first roll

What numbers did Leonardo throw on each roll of the six-sided dice? Was his prediction therefore correct?

Figuratively Speaking

Busy in his workshop, Leonardo was putting the finishing touches to a sketch of what would eventually become a large religious mural. It would be constructed of four sections side by side, each featuring a different figure from the bible. Each of these sections would have a different dominant shade.

He chose four apprentices to assist him with the final product, with one helping with each section. In order that they prepare the right pigments for their sections, Leonardo gave his four apprentices the following notes:

- Angelo would work on the leftmost section
- Marco's section would depict Saint Mark
- The blue section would depict Mary
- Lorenzo would work on the green section
- The orange section would be the rightmost
- Lorenzo would work on the section to the right of the red section
- Antonio's section would feature the archangel Michael
- The section third from the left would feature Saint John
- The image of archangel Michael would be neither the leftmost nor the rightmost section

Which section would each apprentice paint, and which shade would each predominantly use?

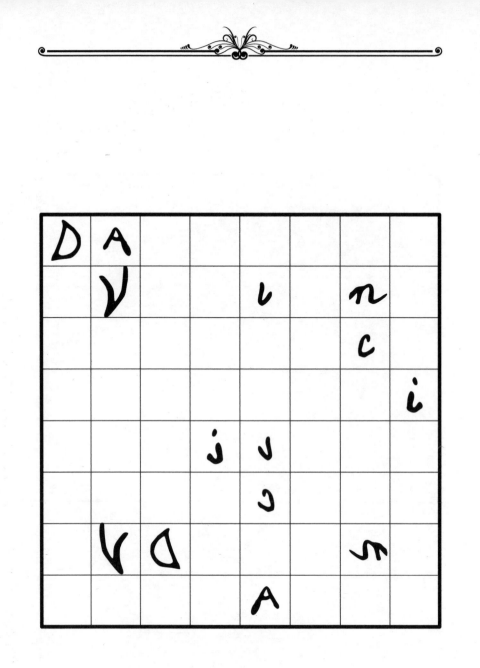

The Mirror Link

Leonardo's apprentices decided to create some exercises for themselves so that they might read their master's personal notes more easily, most of which had been written backwards.

In the exercise opposite, each of the letters must be linked to its exact mirror image. Can you do so by joining the letters into pairs using a series of separate paths, one per pair? Paths must only travel horizontally or vertically from square to square, and no more than one path can enter any square.

Sculptural Challenge

In his workshop, Leonardo had been working on sketches for a large painting commissioned by a benefactor, which was to depict a contemporary victory in battle. In particular, the image needed to feature several horses and their riders.

Ever the student of anatomy, Leonardo decided to create small sculptures of the three horses which he wished to paint in most detail, in order to understand their form more fully.

He created three models, with one of each horse. The models were each made from different materials, and each horse was depicted in a different pose from the others.

- The horse sculpted in a galloping pose was not the figure made from plaster
- The horse that would feature in the middle of the painting was created in clay
- The wax sculpture depicted a bucking horse
- The horse sculpted as standing still would be shown on the right of the painting

What was the sculpture that would appear on the left of the painting made of, and what pose was this horse shown in?

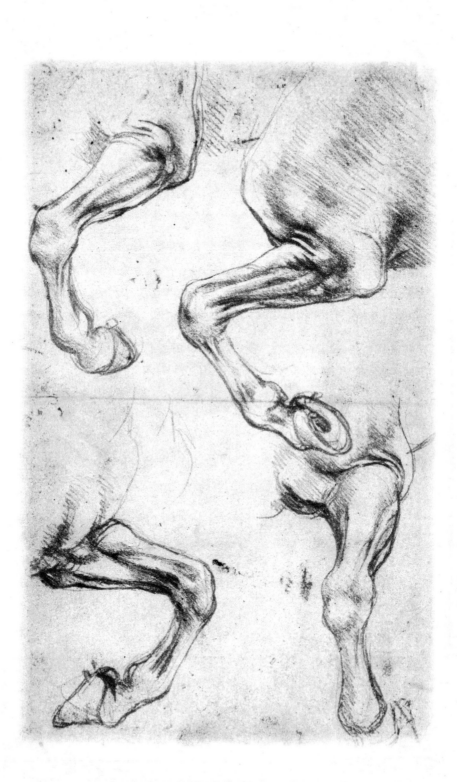

A Dicey Game 3

In his workshop, Leonardo was rolling a regular six-sided dice. He continued to make notes on the results of his throws, so that he might compare the outcomes against the probabilities he expected.

According to his latest prediction, if he rolled the dice six times, then the same number of odd as even numbers would appear.

At the end of his third experiment, he had written the following notes:

- The sum of the second and fourth numbers was the same as the product of those numbers
- The sum of the first and second numbers equalled the sum of the third and sixth numbers
- The sixth number was exactly double the value of the second number
- The value of the fifth number was lower than that of the third number

His prediction turned out to be correct, so what numbers did Leonardo throw on each roll of the six-sided dice?

The Cover of Darkness

Leonardo had been studying the effects of natural light on rocks and trees, so that he might more accurately depict them in the backgrounds of his portraits.

He made a note of the exact time of sunset each day for a month, during the period when the days were growing longer toward the middle of the year. In that particular month, he noted that the sunset was 2 minutes and 8 seconds later every day than the day before.

This particular month had five Sundays. If the sun set at exactly 6:40 pm on the first Sunday of the month, at what time did it set on the fifth Sunday?

Signature Sketch

Leonardo da Vinci had just put the finishing touches to a design for a new military weapon, created according to his commission by the head of a friendly city-state.

Leonardo did not want his plans to fall into enemy hands, however, so he set about making decoy copies of his sketches. He drew a small but crucial error onto each of four decoy copies, and signed them all with his name—but in each case he made a small change to his signature so that he would be able to readily identify the fake copies at any future point.

Can you identify the difference in his signature on each four of the decoy signatures opposite? Each signature has a different change, so you should be able to identify the changes by comparing against the other three signatures in each case.

l. DA Vinci 1507

l. DA Vinci 1507

l. DA Vinci 1507

l. DA Vinci 1507

Not Born Yesterday

One of Leonardo's apprentices asked his master what year he had been born in.

That eminent master replied:

> "The digits in the year of my birth sum to a number formed of two consecutive digits. Call that number Y. This number is the product of two consecutive numbers.

> "Subtract Y from the year I was born, then divide your new number by Y, and divide it by Y again, and the number remaining is 10."

Given that he was born in the 15th century, then in which precise year was Leonardo da Vinci born?

Dizzy Heights

When creating *The Vitruvian Man*, Leonardo measured the heights of three of his apprentices and assessed their relative proportions.

- Luca and Mauro's combined height was a total of 335 cm
- Mauro and Giorgio's combined height was a total of 353 cm
- Giorgio and Luca's combined height was a total of 346 cm

What height was each apprentice, and what was the difference in height between the shortest and tallest of the three?

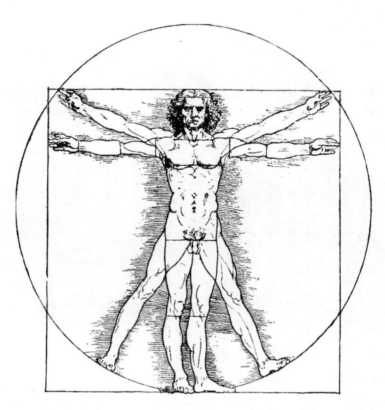

Aerial View 1

Leonard da Vinci was taking a walk around the walled city of Imola. He studied the buildings and streets closely, with the intention of making an aerial map. A bird's-eye view of the city would be invaluable for the city's ruler from a strategic military perspective, and such maps were extremely rare in the field of mapmaking.

From the corner of the city's main square, Leonardo saw the following complex building arrangement from street level:

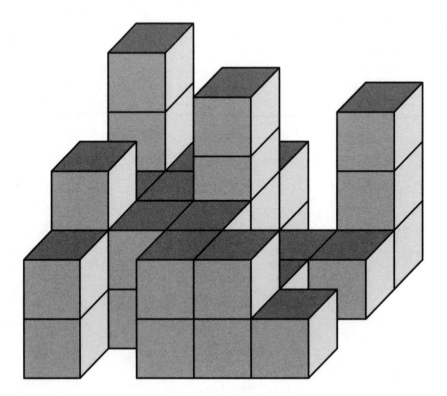

Which of the options below, A–E, shows how Leonardo should draw the building from above onto his bird's-eye-view map?

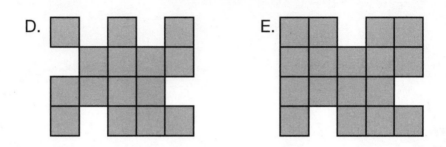

Get in Gear

Leonardo had been studying mechanical principles of movement, in order to create a new machine. In a recent sketch, he had begun to explore how multiple gear wheels and cables might be connected in pairs to create a device capable of lifting extremely heavy loads. He asked his workshop to make a prototype machine based on the series of linked wheels he had set out in his plans. Unfortunately for his apprentices, however, he had left the sketch incomplete.

In the unfinished sketch opposite, each of the gear wheels must be linked to its identical partner. Can you do so by joining the wheels into pairs using a series of separate paths, one per pair? Paths must only travel horizontally or vertically from square to square, and no more than one path can enter any square.

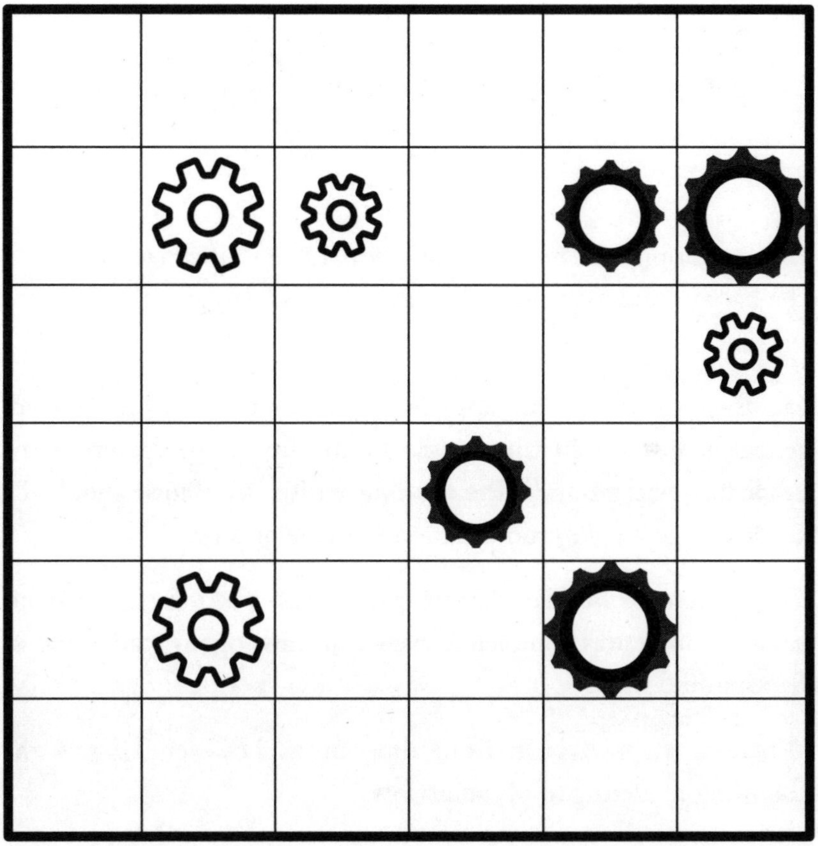

The Apprentice's Graduation

In preparation for a new portrait, Leonardo da Vinci had painted in the background of his canvas with a gradual darkening toward the bottom.

He then instructed an apprentice to paint a flat, mid-toned, rectangular block in the middle of the image, overpainting the graduated background. The shading within the block should be completely even, with no variation in shade or tone.

The apprentice worked close to the canvas, making sure that his solid rectangle was completely even and showing no graduation of depth in the paint.

When he stepped back from the canvas, however, he saw the following rendering of his paintwork:

Not wanting to displease Leonardo, he added more paint to the rectangle until he was sure it was completely evenly coated in paint. But when he stepped back again, the problem still remained.

Why was he unable to create an even block with the paint that he had?

Abandoned Works

Leonardo had recently created three detailed sketches which would eventually become three different commissioned portraits. When one of the commissioners appeared in the workshop one day to check on progress, Leonardo sent an apprentice to fetch the sketch of the relevant portrait.

The apprentice noticed the following details about the three sketches:

- Lucretia's portrait was not the one which had a background of pine trees
- The pastel sketch was beneath the one which had a background of cypress trees
- Cecilia's sketch had been finished with oils
- The sketch drawn in ink had a background of olive trees
- The sketch carrying the label "Beatrice" was created with pastels

Leonardo had asked him to fetch the sketch featuring the background of cypress trees. Who did this portrait depict?

Geared Up 1

Leonardo da Vinci had designed a prototype for a self-propelling cart, which primarily used coiled springs as its source of power. The springs powered a series of gears that connected parts of the cart together and pushed it forward.

In the design opposite, several gears are laid out, forming a chain of motion.

If gear A were to spin clockwise, which direction would gear B spin: clockwise or counterclockwise?

The Draw

Leonardo had space in his workshop for a new apprentice, and had devised a creative way to determine who to appoint as his newest student.

In total, sixteen young artists applied for the position. Leonardo determined that the candidates should be split into pairs, with each pair to draw the same still-life scene. In each pair, he would choose which sketch had been superior; its creator would then face a new artist—the winner of a different pair—and the less successful sketcher would be eliminated from the process.

How many sketches would be produced in total as a result of the contest, if a single winner were to be declared using this method?

Age is Just a Number

Leonardo had three apprentices in his studio, all of whom were helping him to prepare for a large oil portrait. The three apprentices were all different ages.

- Aldo was twice the age now that Dante had been seven years ago
- Ottavio was not the youngest apprentice
- The difference between Ottavio and Dante's current ages was one-eighth of Ottavio's current age
- In five years' time, Ottavio would be one year older than Aldo's current age
- The oldest apprentice was currently 28

When the commission was complete, Leonardo decided that his apprentices should each be paid according to their age, as it reflected the number of years of experience they had brought to the project.

If each apprentice was given a bronze coin for every year of their age, then what was each of the apprentices paid?

A State of Amazement

Leonardo da Vinci sometimes became frustrated with the city he lived in. Far from the wide piazzas and organized grid layout he had designed for his ideal city, the buildings formed a complex labyrinth of narrow, winding passages. There were several dead ends, which made navigating the streets a difficult task.

In fact, there was only one complete route through the city from the north gate to the south gate, and it was certainly not a direct one.

Can you draw it in on the map opposite?

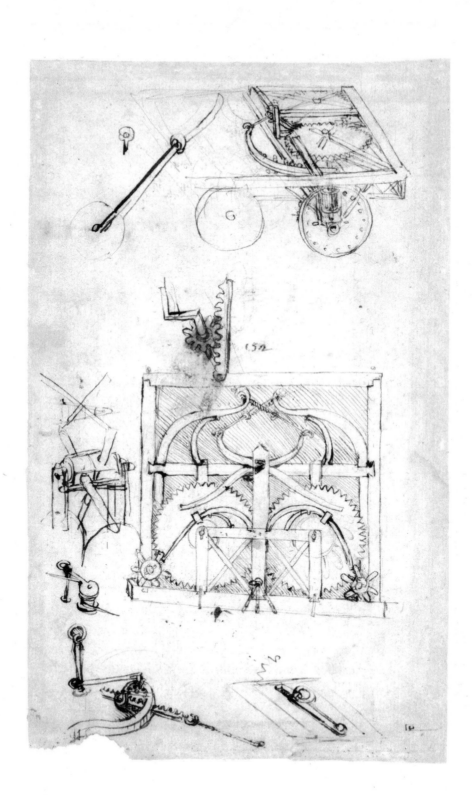

The Head Start

Leonardo da Vinci had created two prototypes for self-propelling vehicles. One of these was powered with springs, while the other used steam pressure.

He decided to race the two machines next to one another along a straight alleyway, and marked out a distance of 12 m for the devices to race from start to finish.

After the first race, it was noted that the spring-loaded vehicle was slower than the steam-powered one, having moved at four-fifths of its speed. Leonardo calculated that the slower device moved at 40 cm per second.

For the second race, he decided to release the spring-loaded device first, and then release the steam-powered device 6 seconds later.

Assuming both vehicles progressed at the same speeds as during the previous race, which device would reach the finish line first?

Pulley the Other One

In his sketchbook, Leonardo da Vinci had begun to design a large robot-like machine which worked with a system of cables and pulleys. He had drawn the wheels needed for each pulley to work, but had left the workshop before drawing in any of the cables, and the plan was therefore incomplete.

Each of the white wheels needed to be connected to a shaded wheel with a single cable, and each cable needed to be either horizontal or vertical. None of the cables could cross over one another, nor cross another wheel, or the system would become jammed.

Can you join the wheels with cables to complete the plan, so that all the wheels are joined into pairs, with one shaded and one white wheel per pair?

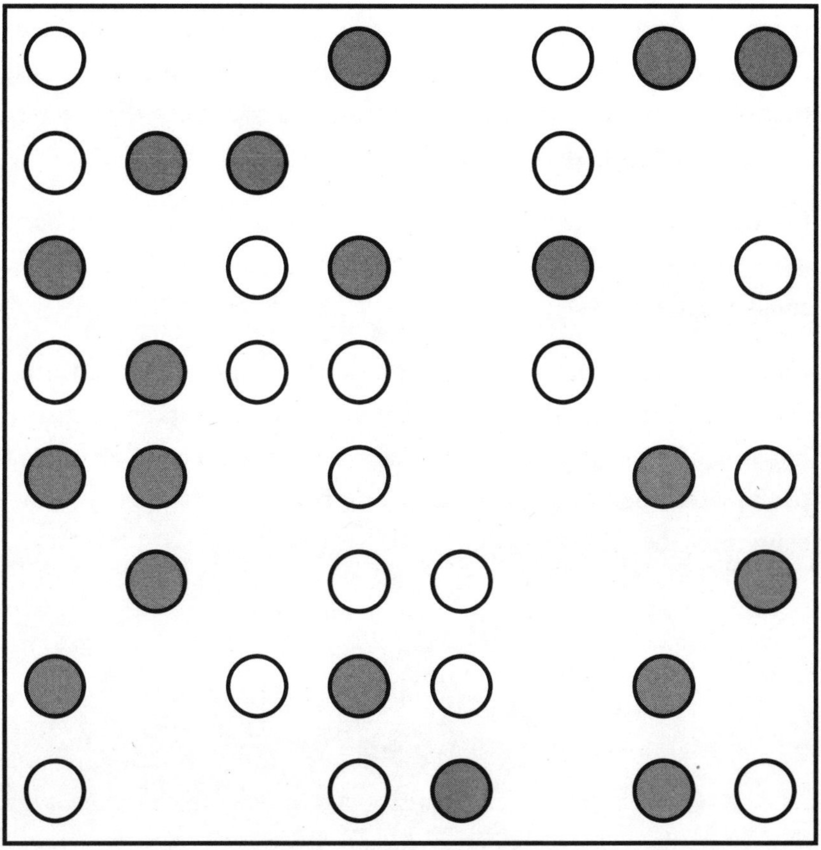

The Water Fountains

In creating the designs for his ideal city, Leonardo was careful to make sure that clean water was available to all citizens. He decided that water fountains should be spread around the city so that no area was geographically disadvantaged in terms of its water supply.

On the sketch of the city below, distinct residential areas have been delineated with bold lines, with each area then split into several smaller grid squares.

Can you place exactly two water fountains into each residential area on the plan, so that no two fountains are in adjacent squares, not even diagonally? No more than one fountain may be placed per square. There must also be exactly two fountains per row and column of the grid.

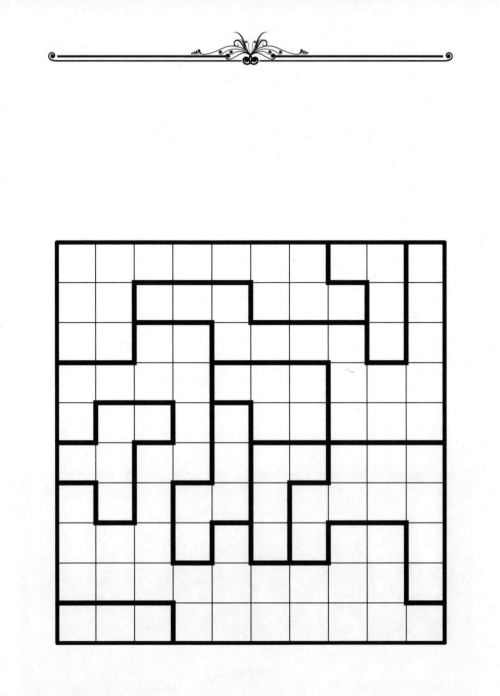

Ahead of his Time

Two of Leonardo da Vinci's apprentices were discussing their master's work on *The Last Supper*. They noted that the work had taken him several years to complete, from the first sketches to the final piece.

One of the apprentices asked their master what age he had been when he had finally finished the mural.

Leonardo replied:

> "My age then was a two-digit number, which was itself five times the sum of its digits."

What age was Leonardo when he completed *The Last Supper*?

Multi-faceted Problem

Leonardo had been honing his skill for drawing regular geometric shapes. While in the middle of a certain drawing, one of his assistants asked which particular shape he was sketching.

"It's a triakontakaihexagon," replied his master.

The apprentice confessed that he did not know the term, and asked how many sides the polygon would have.

His master replied:

"The number of sides is a two-digit square number, which increases by three-quarters of its value when the digits are reversed."

How many sides would the completed polygon have?

Aerial View 2

Leonardo was adding more buildings to his map of the city of Imola. From a particular vantage point, he observed this view of a fortified building within the city walls:

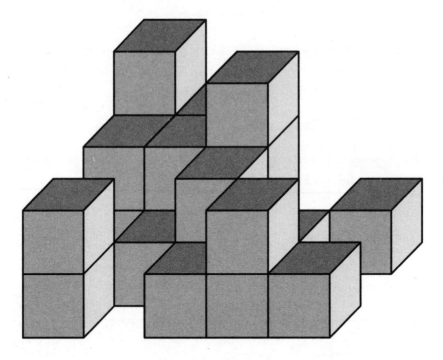

Which of the options below, A–E, would be the most accurate representation of the building when pictured from a bird's-eye view?

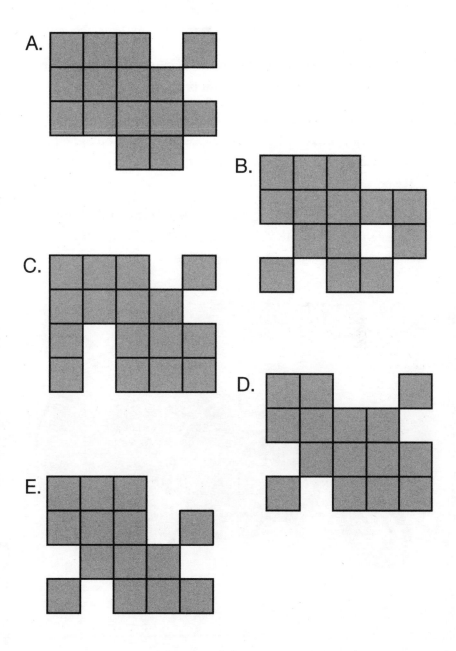

To Coin a Phrase

Leonardo was in need of new pigment supplies, so he went to fetch the money bag he kept in his workshop.

There were three types of coin in use in the city-state in which he lived: bronze, silver, and gold. A bronze coin could buy one pot of pigment, a silver coin could buy two pots, and a gold coin could buy three pots.

Leonardo looked in the bag and saw that he had two coins with which he would be able to buy five pots of pigment. Neither coin was silver, however. How was this possible?

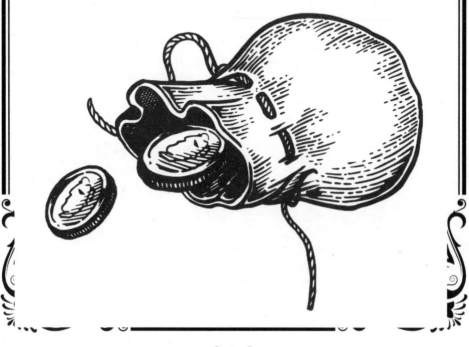

Time and Dedication

Leonardo was looking through a recently completed sketchbook to see how much space he had previously dedicated to particular topics during his studies.

He saw that for every page dedicated to anatomical studies, there were three pages with designs for flying inventions, two pages of mountain sketches, and one page of purely mathematical calculations.

There were 84 pages in the notebook. How many pages were dedicated to flying inventions?

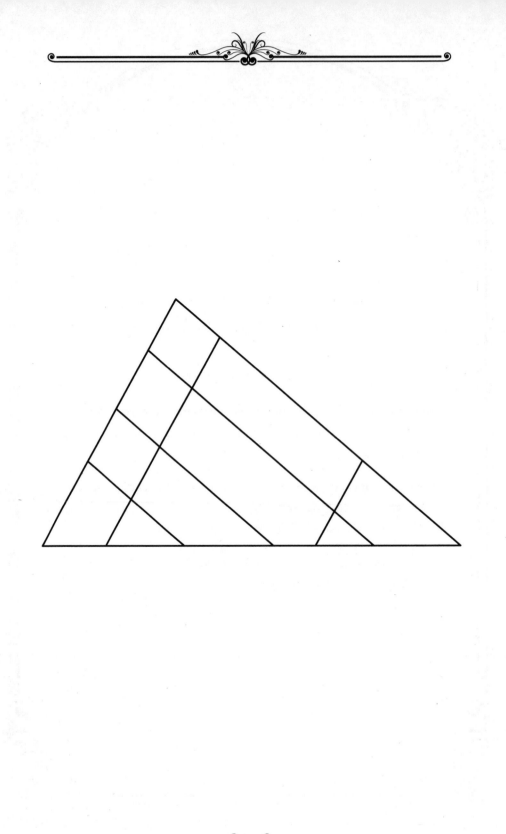

Triangulation Problem

Looking up at the ceiling of the roof of a benefactor, Leonardo da Vinci noticed a stained-glass panel which allowed light into the room. It had been irregularly lined with lead, creating an unusual geometric pattern, shown opposite.

One of Leonardo's apprentices commented that there were an unusual number of quadrilateral areas created by the window, to which another replied that there were clearly many more triangles than quadrilaterals in the configuration.

Including the outer perimeter, are there more triangles or quadrilaterals in the window?

Exploded View 1

Leonardo da Vinci's notebooks were filled with complicated plans for devices, machines, and vehicles. Fortunately for his apprentices, the designs were often drawn alongside an "exploded view", meaning that the small parts of the machine were sketched out separately to show how the whole device could be pieced together.

Leonardo set his apprentices a challenge to see which of them could draw the constituent parts of the machine he had created.

Which of the four apprentices created the only correct "exploded view" of the construction shown at the top? The correct option should contain neither more nor less pieces than are needed to make the construction as shown

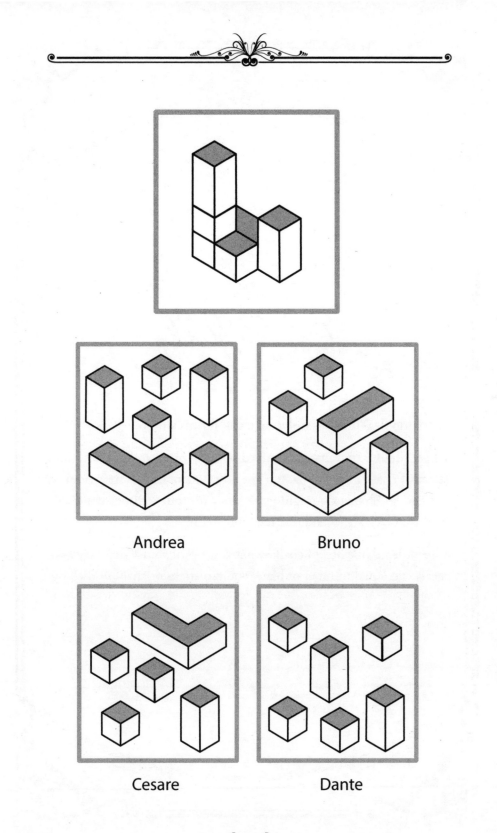

Andrea

Bruno

Cesare

Dante

Chalk It Up

Leonardo da Vinci was ordering chalk for his studio.

Chalk could be purchased in mixed boxes of black and red, with four sticks of chalk in each box, but the amounts of each were randomly chosen. So, Leonardo might get a box with four red sticks of chalk, or three black sticks and one red, and so on.

If he ordered one box of chalk, what is the probability that he would receive an equal number of black and red sticks of chalk in the box?

Out of all Proportion

Leonardo was studying the anatomical form of an eagle that happened to be nesting in the roof above his workshop.

He noticed that the eagle's claw was 10 cm in length, which was the same as the difference between the bird's wingspan and its length from beak to tailfeather.

If the length of the eagle's claw was one-sixteenth of the total combined measurements of the claw, wingspan, and beak-to-tip lengths, then what was the eagle's wingspan?

Exploded View 2

Disappointed by his apprentices' lack of attention to detail, Leonardo set them another challenge.

Once again, he created a small structure and asked his tutees to create an "exploded view" diagram of the construction, showing each of the constituent parts isolated from one another.

Leonardo's construction is shown at the top. Which of his apprentices was the only one to create a valid "exploded view" of the creation, with no extra parts needed or unnecessary parts shown?

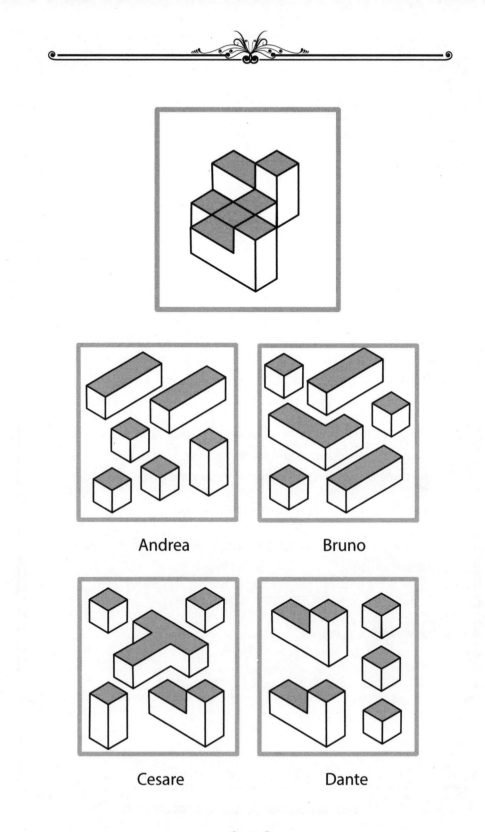

Andrea

Bruno

Cesare

Dante

Secret Sketches

Leonardo had received a commission from a highly respected nobleman to create a portrait of that nobleman's beloved mistress. Given the delicate nature of the subject, Leonardo encoded the name of the mistress in his notes, so that he might not accidentally reveal her name to society and embroil her in an unnecessary scandal.

He had invented a system of encoding so that nobody passing through the workshop could easily discover her name. His own name, using the same encryption, would be written as follows:

Ovlmziwl wz Ermxr

The mistress's name, encoded in Leonardo's sketchbook, was similarly written like this:

Xvxrorz Tzoovizmr

What was her real name?

Clearing Out

Leonardo had come to the end of a commission, and wanted to take stock of the art supplies in his workshop. At the beginning of the project, he had originally had 68 full glass pots—some were filled with paint and some were filled with ink.

By the end of the project, 14 of the ink pots had been emptied, and three-quarters of the paint pots were empty. He had also been left with twice as many full paint pots as full ink pots, and all of the original pots were now either full or empty—so there were no part-full pots.

How many full glass ink pots had been in the workshop at the beginning of the project?

Pots and Lids

· • • ·

Leonardo's apprentices looked around his workshop and realized that it had become very disorganized.

None of the paint pots had their lids attached, meaning the precious paints would dry out and have to be re-mixed. To prevent accidental mixing of pigments, each pot had its own lid, which should not be mixed up with a different pair.

On the workbench opposite, each of the dark pots needs to be matched to exactly one light lid. Match up the pots and lids by drawing straight lines to form pairs, ensuring the lines are only horizontal or vertical—so no diagonal lines. To prevent cross-contamination, lines should not cross another line, another pot, or a lid.

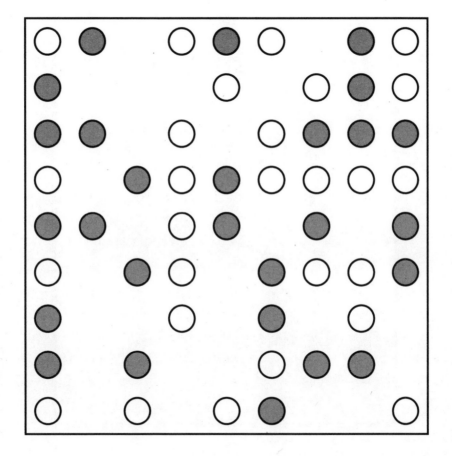

The Family Tree Fee

Leonardo da Vinci was commissioned to create miniature portraits of each of the male members of a noble house for whom he was contracted. He was promised one gold coin for each of the portraits he completed.

Within the one household, there was one great-grandfather, two grandfathers, four fathers, five sons, two uncles, two brothers, two nephews, two first cousins, three grandsons, one great-uncle, one great-nephew, and one great-grandson. All of these listed relationships pertained exclusively to members within the household.

If Leonardo were to indeed create a portrait for each and every male member of the household, what is the minimum number of gold coins he could expect to earn for his work?

In Leonardo da Vinci's workshop, the following sequence had been scribbled into a notebook:

$$9999 = 9$$

$$8888 = 5$$

$$7777 = 1$$

$$6666 = 6$$

$$999 = 9$$

$$888 = 6$$

$$777 = 3$$

$$666 = ?$$

Leonardo came across the notebook and was bemused as to what the author's intention had been.

Can you work out how each of these equivalences has been calculated, and therefore say what single digit should replace the question mark on the final line?

Number Sets 2

In his notebook, Leonardo da Vinci wrote out several numbers, organized into sets as follows:

Set 1

4   9   16

Set 2

1   64

Set 3

8   27   125

What rules had Leonardo used to organize the numbers into these sets?

Silver Areas

Leonardo was holding a workshop on the juxtaposition of white and black paints on the same canvas. In particular, he wanted his students to notice how a silver tone sometimes appeared when white paint was applied on top of black paint.

He showed his tutees the canvas opposite, where he had painted a brilliant white grid across a pure black background.

He pointed out that where the white lines crossed, the image of a small circle appeared at the join. How many of those small circles had he painted silver, and how many were actually white?

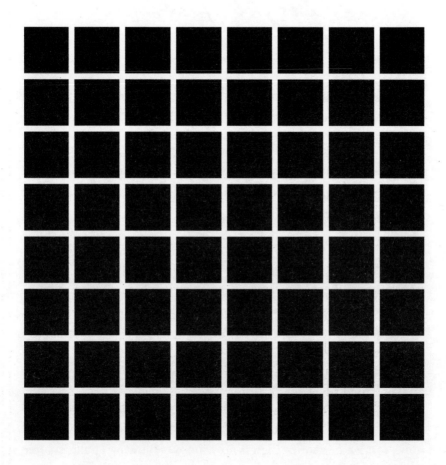

Flight Pattern

Leonardo da Vinci had been studying the effects of the wind on a bird's ability to fly.

He observed an eagle making its way back and forth across the sky, collecting materials for its huge nest. It would fly directly north from its nest, gather what it needed from a nearby wood, and then fly due south again to return to its nesting spot.

Leonardo observed the eagle over the course of a day, and noted that it faced a strong headwind when flying north, but that it profited from an equally strong tailwind when flying back south again. As such, the bird flew more slowly when flying north despite expending the same amount of energy as flying south, when it flew faster thanks to the tailwind.

If the bird flew from its nest to the forest and back again ten times over the course of a day, and the wind blew at a constant speed and direction, would the overall time taken to make the journeys be the same, longer, or shorter than if no wind was blowing at all? Assume that the bird flies with the same amount of effort, regardless of the wind speed or the load it carries.

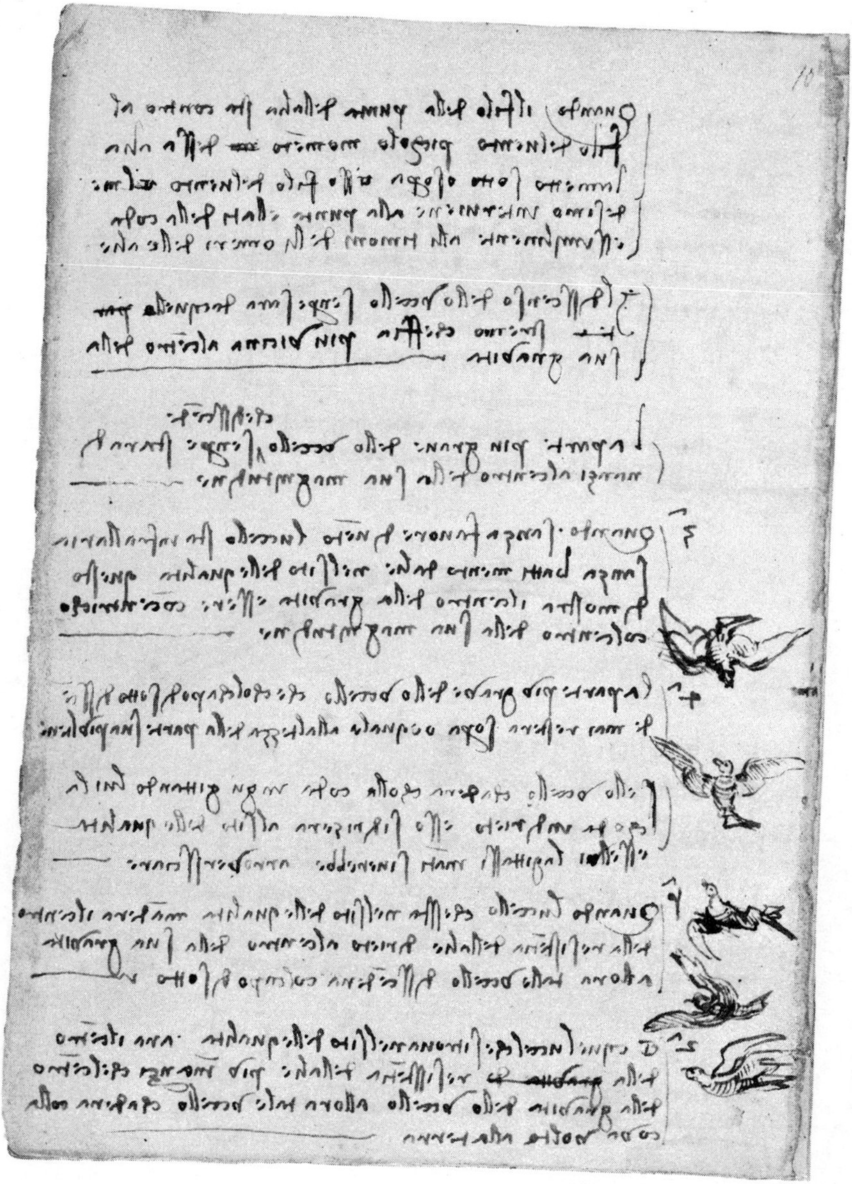

The Outposts

As part of his military consultancy for a patron, Leonardo da Vinci had designed a weapon capable of firing multiple cannons almost simultaneously.

In order to tempt the patron to order many of these devices, Leonardo wanted to show how they might be placed strategically around a city to ensure that no area was ever too far from a defensive weapon.

On the plan of the city opposite, distinct military zones have been outlined in bold, and then split into smaller squares. Can you place a cannon into some squares so that there are exactly two cannons in every military zone, and no cannons are in adjacent squares, including diagonally? No more than one cannon may be placed per square. There must also be exactly two cannons per row and column of the grid.

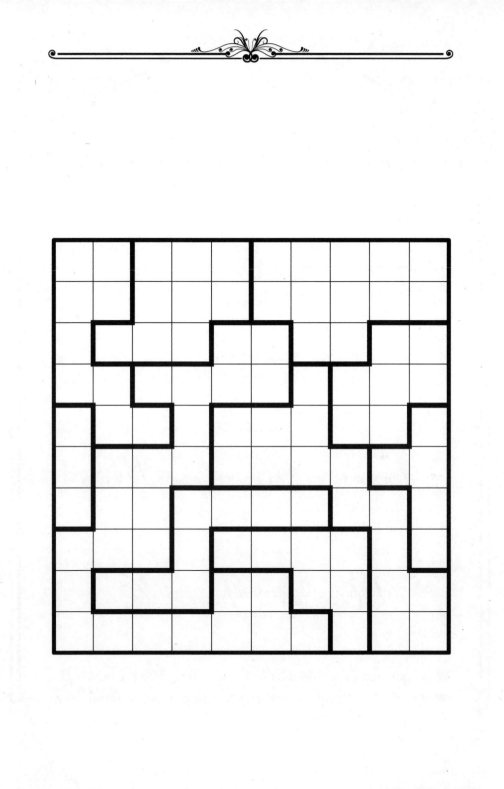

Connections Conundrum 1

One night, Leonardo wrote out a series of names in his sketchbook, and then organized them into the following sets:

Set A:

Earth

Set A + B:

Venus Mercury Mars

Set B:

Minerva Juno Ceres

What rule had Leonardo da Vinci used to organize the names into these sets? Nowadays Uranus could be added to Set A, but it wasn't known during Leonardo da Vinci's lifetime.

The Whole Dam Problem

As a military strategist, Leonardo da Vinci had been speaking with his Florentine patron about the best way of bringing destruction to the rival city of Pisa.

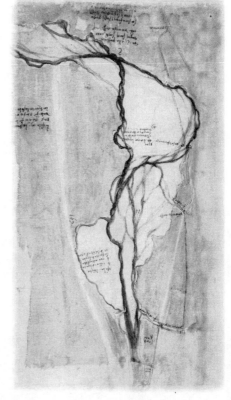

The chief topic of their discussion had been the Arno river, which flowed through the city of Florence and then continued west to Pisa before eventually reaching the sea. The strategists thought that if they could stop the river from reaching Pisa, it would cut off Pisa's primary water supply and therefore force the entire city into ruin.

One of Leonardo's apprentices suggested creating a dam just outside the west edge of Florence, after it had flowed through the city, to prevent it flowing further downstream and reaching Pisa.

Why would creating such a dam not be the most sensible course of action for the strategists?

Geared Up 2

In his role as a military engineer, Leonardo da Vinci designed a rolling, rotating bridge which could be used by infantry forces to speed up river crossings.

In the sketch below, a series of gears are used to raise and lower the bridge. When the gear marked A is turned clockwise, the bridge is lowered.

When the gear marked B is turning clockwise, is the bridge being lowered or being raised?

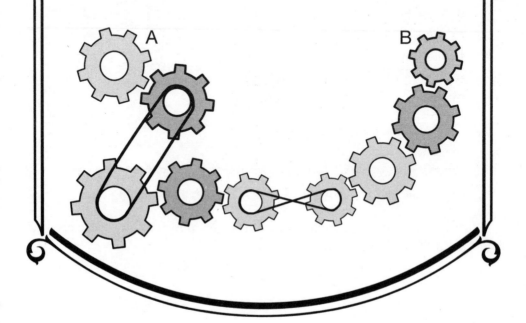

Into the Fold

Leonardo da Vinci moved to France at the request of the French King, while he was still working on his famous portrait of Lisa del Giocondo. While packing up his workshop, he asked his apprentice to make sure the unfinished portrait was properly loaded to be taken to the palace.

Leonardo watched as his apprentice folded up the canvas and carefully rolled it between layers of cotton to preserve the paint.

He could tell, however, that it was not the *Mona Lisa* that had been packed, but another painting entirely.

How might he know that his apprentice had packed up the wrong painting?

Exploded View 3

Leonardo set his apprentices a final challenge, to see whether or not they had improved their diagrammatic skills.

He created the structure on the left (below) from a series of wooden blocks, and asked his apprentices to create a diagram of it using an "exploded view"—that is, showing the constituent blocks separately from one another.

Which one of the apprentices managed to create an "exploded view" of the structure on the left, without including any unnecessary extra pieces?

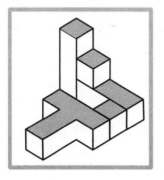

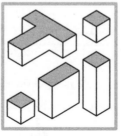

Andrea

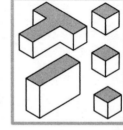

Bruno

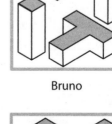

Cesare

Dante

Number Sets 3

In his notebook, Leonardo da Vinci wrote out the digits from 1 to 9, and then organized them into sets as follows:

Set 1

6　8　9

Set 2

3　2　5

Set 3

1　4　7

What rule had he used to organize the numbers into their sets? He explained that it had nothing to do with the numeric value of each digit.

The Longest Night

Under the watch of his patron, Leonardo had designed a mechanical rolling bridge that could be swung out over rivers and streams to give military forces access to locations which would otherwise be impossible—or at least very slow—to reach.

He asked his workshop to create a prototype, and the patron then asked Leonardo to test out the device over a small stream to see how sturdy it was.

Not wanting any enemy spies to see the proposed device in case they picked up in advance on the advantages it would offer, the patron asked that the experiment be conducted after dark.

The patron proposed conducting the test after the shortest day of the year, to give the engineer as much time as possible to test the device under the cover of night.

When it came to this test, however, it was realized that the device was not actually needed to cross the chosen stream after all. Why might that have been the case?

Order of Magnitude

Leonardo was in the process of ordering more ink for his workshop.

The black and red ink would be delivered in different-sized pots, with black ink in the larger size pot. A single crate of ink could therefore fit seven pots of black ink, or nine pots of red ink.

Leonardo ordered several boxes, each with either only red or only black ink pots inside. He made sure he had more black ink pots than red ink pots, and only ordered full boxes.

Overall, he received 62 pots of ink in his order.

How many pots of red ink did he order?

Leonardo was putting the finishing touches to his map of Imola, and observed the following view of a building at the gated entrance to the city:

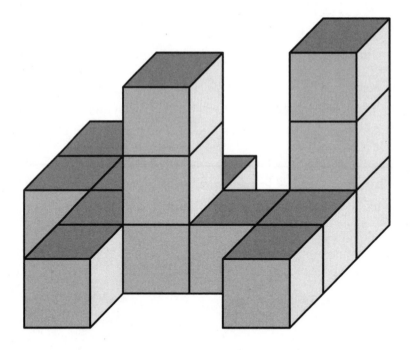

Which of the options below, A–E, shows how he should represent the building on his map, using a bird's-eye view?

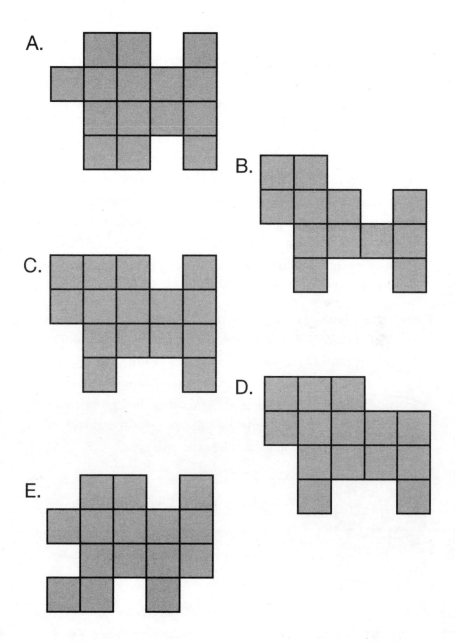

A.

B.

C.

D.

E.

The Missing Coins

After being paid a hefty sum for a commission, Leonardo da Vinci decided to give his three apprentices a bonus. He gave each of them six bronze coins to spend however they wished, making a total of eighteen bronze coins in all.

The three men went to a local tavern, and spent the whole of their combined bonus on food and drink. The proprietor, recognizing the young men and acknowledging the fame of their tutor, then came over to their table and gave them back a discount of four bronze coins in total. The young men decided to keep one of these four bronze coins each, and left the final coin on the table for the young waiter who had brought their food.

When they returned to the workshop, however, the three men noticed that there had been a discrepancy in their calculations. They had each effectively paid five coins to the tavern, and left one on

the table for the young waiter—which made a total of sixteen coins. But given that they originally gave the proprietor eighteen coins, where had the extra two gone?

One of the apprentices mentioned the conundrum to their tutor, Leonardo.

What do you think was his master's response? Can you explain where the missing coins had gone?

Frame of Mind

Leonardo had—at long last—finished a commissioned portrait that had required a particularly large amount of effort, and was busy creating a frame for his masterpiece.

He was making a frame out of wood, and had cut and then carved two vertical pieces of wood which would make the sides of the frame. He fixed them into place. When he came to attach a bottom piece, however, it had clearly been cut too long, and would not fit between the two fixed vertical planks. The bottom piece is shown as a pale angled line here:

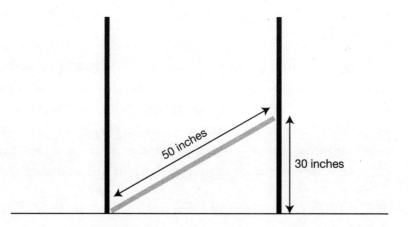

Looking at the lengths marked on the diagram above, how much should Leonardo take off the length of the angled piece so that it would fit snugly in a flat, horizontal direction between the two vertical pieces?

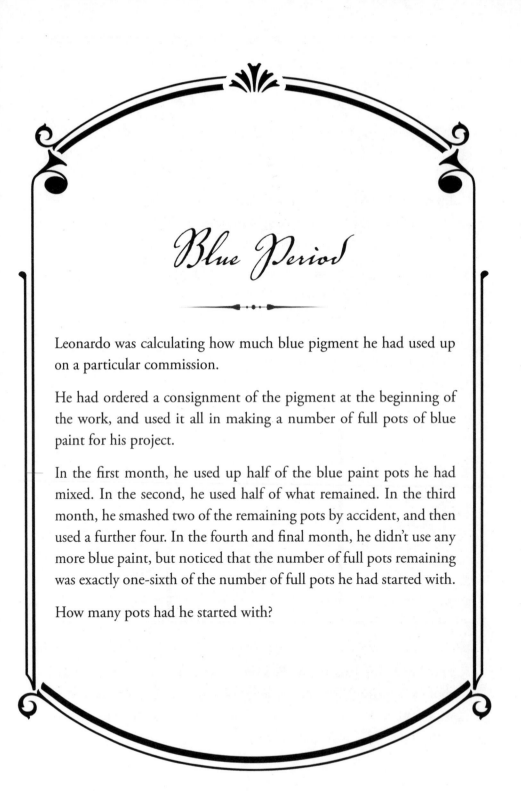

Blue Period

Leonardo was calculating how much blue pigment he had used up on a particular commission.

He had ordered a consignment of the pigment at the beginning of the work, and used it all in making a number of full pots of blue paint for his project.

In the first month, he used up half of the blue paint pots he had mixed. In the second, he used half of what remained. In the third month, he smashed two of the remaining pots by accident, and then used a further four. In the fourth and final month, he didn't use any more blue paint, but noticed that the number of full pots remaining was exactly one-sixth of the number of full pots he had started with.

How many pots had he started with?

Spring into Action

Leonardo da Vinci's designs for a spring-loaded cart were being finalized. Central to its mechanism were two large springs which powered the forward motion of the cart, releasing energy as they gradually uncoiled.

Unfortunately for Leonardo, the two springs were not an infinite source of power, and the cart would start to lose speed as the springs expanded further and further.

Leonardo set up a test course outside his workshop, and, using a small model prototype of the cart, fully loaded the springs. He then released the cart in order to observe how rapidly the deceleration affected the progress of his device.

In the first second after being released, the cart moved forward 1 yard. For each subsequent second, however, the cart moved only half as far as it had in the previous second.

How long would it take for the cart to travel over 2 yards?

The Great Divide

Leonardo da Vinci had been commissioned to paint a fresco on the wall of a new benefactor's house. The area to be painted was a perfect square, with a total area of 9 square yards.

Leonardo had three apprentices working to prepare the wall before the painting could commence.

The three apprentices were different ages, and Leonardo had observed how the apprentices brought more experience to the project as their ages increased. Leonardo therefore wanted the oldest apprentice to show the youngest how to prepare the wall, deciding that they should both prepare a perfectly square area of the wall, with the youngest apprentice preparing a quarter of the area that the oldest would cover. These two areas must not overlap.

The remaining apprentice would then prepare all the remaining areas of the wall, though his total area to prepare should be exactly equal to that of the oldest apprentice and should be a continuous area.

What area of the wall should each apprentice cover?

Divisions, Decisions

Leonardo da Vinci had taken on two new apprentices, and allowed them to share an unused workbench in that distinguished artist's studio. The bench was an irregular shape, however, and the two argued over how to divide the working space into two equal parts, so that neither tutee should be disadvantaged.

Suppose that it is possible to draw a single straight line across the desk, to divide its worktop space in two. But with no simple geometric way to divide the irregularly shaped bench in half, what solution could Leonardo propose as a way of the two apprentices fairly dividing the space between themselves, without the need to do any measuring at all?

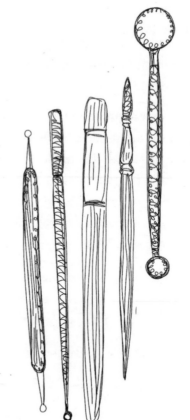

Weights and Measures

During the creation of his self-balancing scale, Leonardo had noticed that the calculations he was making were not consistent. After some investigation, he decided that one of the standard weights he had been using was not, in fact, standard at all.

He had nine iron bars which should have been identical in weight. He suspected, however, that one of them weighed less than the others, and was causing the miscalculations.

He wanted to use his balancing scales, which he knew to be accurate, to determine which of the bars was underweight.

What is the minimum number of uses of the balancing scales that Leonardo would have to undertake in order to establish which one of the iron bars was underweight?

Open Air

Integrated into Leonardo da Vinci's designs for the ideal city were wide, open public areas where people could congregate and travel at their leisure.

On the prototype map of an ideal city opposite, each of the distinct areas has been outlined with a bold line and then split into squares. Can you draw the location of 20 public piazzas onto the grid in such a way that that each area has exactly the same number of piazzas?

Piazzas should not be built in adjacent squares, including diagonally, and no more than one piazza may be placed per square. There must also be exactly two piazzas per row and column of the grid.

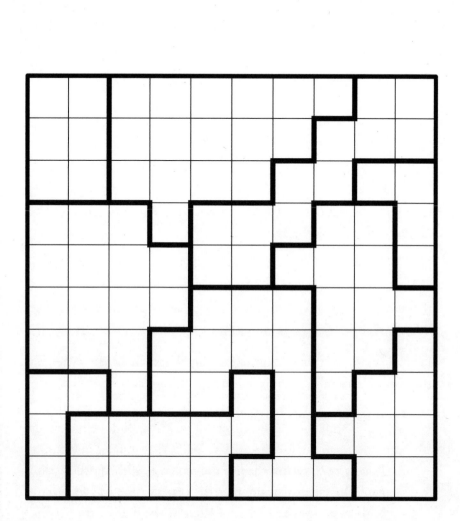

Timing Trouble

Leonardo da Vinci had created two prototype clocks for testing, each with the standard 1 to 12 numerals on their faces. Both of the clocks were powered by springs.

Unfortunately, when tested against an existing clock that he knew to be accurate, neither of the clocks kept the time correctly. One of them was fast, gaining 10 minutes for every hour that elapsed. The other was slow, losing 6 minutes for every hour that elapsed.

He had begun the test at 12 pm, ensuring that each device started on the correct time, and he finished the test 12 hours later.

1. What time was shown on each prototype clock after 12 hours?

2. If he were to re-run the test the next day, what drastic action could he take to ensure that the correct time was shown on both new devices 12 hours later, at the end of the second test run?

Mirrored Magic

In Leonardo da Vinci's studio, two of his apprentices were using a mirror to decipher their master's latest notes, which were of course written backwards.

They noticed that the mirror on the workbench seemed to have what they thought to be a most unusual property: when both men looked directly into the middle of the mirror, they did not see themselves reflected at all, but instead only the other apprentice.

Considering that the mirror was not a supernatural one, how was this possible?

A Material Difference

When creating designs for a parachute, Leonardo experimented with both linen sheets and simple tent structures to help solidify his plans.

Suppose that he wanted to create a tent using only simple apparatus: a single sheet for the floor, a single sheet for the ceiling, and a series of poles to hold up the ceiling in the middle, so that in profile it looked like this:

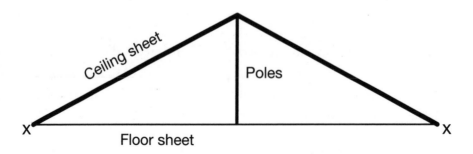

For the creation of his latest tent, he had a ceiling sheet that measured 50 feet by 50 feet (which would be placed with 25 feet either side of the central poles), and a floor sheet that measured 48 feet by 48 feet. He attached the edges of the sheets together with tent pegs at the points marked "X" above. Assume that the two sheets are placed so that their edges run parallel.

Before building the tent, Leonardo told his assembled apprentices that, when propped up with poles as shown opposite, any person could comfortably stand upright in the middle of the resulting tent, without any length being added or removed from either the ceiling or floor sheets.

His apprentices doubted he was correct—but was he? How tall would the poles need to be to create the maximum height in the tallest part of the tent and to keep the ceiling sheet as taut as possible?

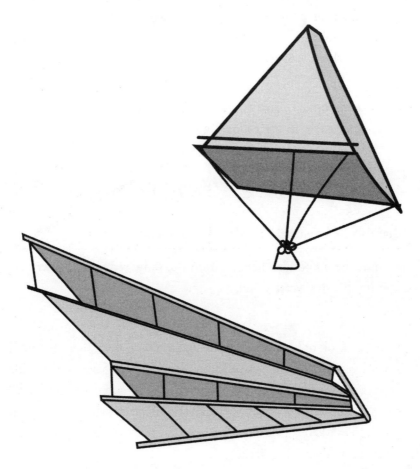

All in a Row

In his sketchbook, Leonardo da Vinci wrote out the numbers from 1 to 15 once each, in the following order:

$$8, 1, 15, 10, 6, 3, 13, 12, 4, 5, 11, 14, 2, 7, 9$$

What rule had he used to order the numbers?

As a hint, he could also have written the same sequence by writing the entire list in reverse order.

A Cut Above

Leonardo had ordered a clay block, from which he wished to make several small sculptures.

The block came in a perfect cube, from which he needed 27 equally sized pieces of clay to make his statues. He asked an apprentice to cut the block into 27 smaller cubes, using a tool that could slice all the way through the block in a single cut.

Given that he would be able to rearrange the pieces after each cut, what is the minimum number of cuts the apprentice would need to make in order to create the 27 cubes?

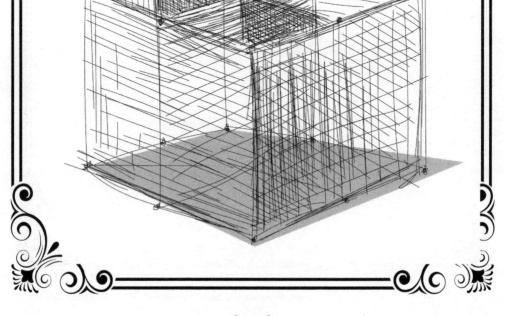

Fair and Square

While studying the mathematical properties of prime numbers, Leonardo da Vinci posed the following question to his apprentices:

"No mean average of any two consecutive prime numbers can be a prime number. But can the mean of two consecutive square numbers have a square root? And if so, what property would be shared by all such possible square roots?"

Notes from the Future

In the creation of his image *The Vitruvian Man*, Leonardo da Vinci looked at the interrelation between the measurements of a square and the measurements of a circle.

In doing so, he referred to a concept from a mathematical problem which had first been written about in 1650.

Leonardo da Vinci, however, died in 1519…

Given that he was not clairvoyant, how could he have accessed the information? Assume that he did not independently discover it, and he learned of it by reading the existing work.

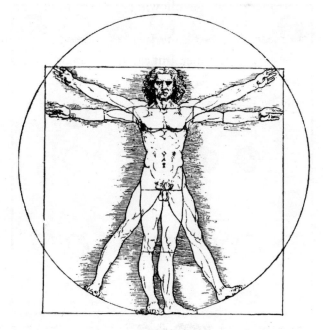

New and full

Leonardo da Vinci was curious about the moon's brilliance, and in particular how it still retained some element of luminance on those areas where the sun did not directly shine.

In the box below are sketches of full and new moons recorded over the course of a year, showing their positions in the night sky. The new and full moons can be joined into pairs, with one of each type in each pair, to represent the beginning and middle of a moon's cycle.

Can you use only straight lines to join the moons into pairs, making sure that all lines are either horizontal or vertical, and ensuring that no lines cross over either one another or any moon?

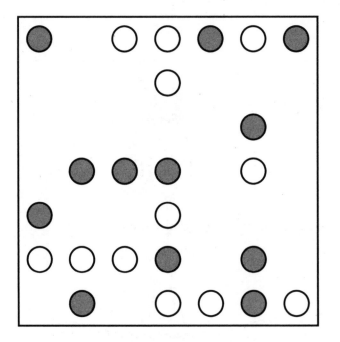

Number Sets 4

In his notebook, Leonardo da Vinci wrote out several numbers, and then organized them into sets as follows:

Set 1

9   12   18

Set 2

3   6   15   21

Set 3

1   10

What rules had he used to organize the numbers into their sets?

Connections Conundrum 2

In his notebook, Leonardo da Vinci wrote out several words, and then organized them into two sets as follows:

Set A

Dodecagon Octagon

Rectangle Square

Set B

Heptagon Nonagon

Pentagon Triangle

What rule had he used to split the shapes into their two sets?

However You Slice It

Leonardo was putting the finishing touches to a mechanical saw. He had built a prototype which could saw a plank of wood in half with a single clean cut, using a complex system of hydraulics.

When the saw was finished, Leonardo fetched a plank from the workshop to test his design.

First, he cut the plank into two halves of exactly the same length. He then cut each of those halves into three equal pieces. Then, from each of those thirds he created five short planks of equal size, before finally cutting each of those fifths into quarters.

How many cuts did Leonardo make in total, and how many pieces had he cut the original plank into by the time he had finished?

Triangulation Points

As part of his mathematical studies, Leonardo da Vinci had been looking at the internal angles of irregular triangles, and observing their geometric relationships to one another.

In one particular triangle he had drawn, the smallest angle was one-fifth of the size of the largest angle. The largest angle was itself two and half times the size of the middle angle, which in turn was twice the size of the smallest angle.

What were the three angles?

Solutions

Walking on Water 1 .... *9*

Olive wood, and with three coats of varnish. In full:

- The smallest model was the one made of pine, which had two coats of varnish.
- The widest model was the one made of olive wood, which had three coats of varnish.
- The longest model was the one made of beech, which had one coat of varnish.

Dipping Point *10*

It would not be correct. If the two spoons of paint moved between the pots were exactly the same size, then no paint is gained or lost between the two pots overall—and also there must be exactly the same amount of paint overall in each pot as there was to begin with. That means that for any amount of red paint in the original blue pot, the exact same amount of blue paint must have been displaced into the original red pot for that to be possible.

The Map *12*

The Tiber. It would still have been the third-longest river in Italy, whether or not Leonardo had drawn it on a map!

The Important Commission *13*

Lisa del Giocondo. The text has been mirrored vertically:

Lisa del Giocondo

The Course of Nature *14*

2 yards. If the apprentice fixed the ruler to a floating pontoon, it would rise as the river levels rose. So, however much the water rose, the ruler would still show the initial height of 2 yards.

A Man of Many Talents *16*

An iris—which is both a flowering plant and the part of the eye surrounding the pupil, as well as the name of the Greek goddess of the rainbow.

Useful Tool 17

A mirror. Leonardo da Vinci was well known for his mirror writing, although he may not have always needed a mirror to write backwards. In any case, a mirror would show you an exact copy of your work, although it is always "turned around"—that is, mirrored.

Flying Machines 18

Alpha: 30 m, 20 kg.

Beta: 40 m, 24 kg.

Gamma: 20 m, 16 kg.

Paint Pigments 20

The pot of ultramarine: although it was almost empty, it was mixed most recently. The lapis pot was the fullest and mixed second, and the cobalt pot was half-full but mixed first.

Something Does Not Add Up 21

364913. Each of the solutions can be split into three sections: the square of the first number, followed by the square of the second number, and finally the sum of the first two numbers. For example, 495 is 2^2 (i.e. 4), followed by 3^2 (i.e. 9), followed by the sum of 2 and 3 (i.e. 5).

Following this pattern, 6 + 7 would result in 364913, since 6^2 = 36, 7^2 = 49, and 6+7 = 13.

Fresh Fresco 22

24 hours. The more experienced apprentice would only need an additional four hours to do all of the work completed by the novice, meaning that in the eight hours they worked together he completed two-thirds of the preparation and worked twice as fast as the novice. Working alone, the novice would therefore take twice as much time as his senior to complete the whole wall: 24 hours.

Anatomy Conundrum 25

The sartorius, which is found in the leg and was the first muscle to be shown. Conversely, the latissimus dorsi muscles are found in the chest, are the widest muscles, and were the second to be shown. The gluteus maximus is found in the buttocks, is the heaviest muscle, and was the third to be shown.

A Series of Events 26

He should copy out the third scrap. All of the four scraps are number sequences given in mirror writing, a common practice of Leonardo da Vinci.

The undamaged sequence remaining on the page, when written normally, shows the following:

0112358

They are the first seven numbers of the Fibonacci sequence, where each number is the sum of the two preceding numbers: 0, 1, 1, 2, 3, 5, 8. The next numbers in the sequence would be 13, 21, 34—which are shown in the third sequence, when the digits are mirrored as below. Evidently Leonardo had missed out the spaces between consecutive numbers:

0112358132134

Petals and Stems 28
7 roses and 5 violets.

A Perfect Sphere 29
It is a certainty—any three marks made on a sphere will always all be in the same hemisphere (assuming you can choose any half of the sphere to form that hemisphere). In the most extreme case, all three might be equidistant along a given "equator" of such a sphere—but could still all be contained in the same hemisphere.

A Mountainous Task 30
The first sketch depicted a hailstorm. It was made at dusk, using ink.

The second sketch depicted a snowstorm. It was made in the morning, using chalk.

The third sketch depicted a rainstorm. It was made at midday, using oils.

A Handy Tip 32
Leonardo was left-handed, so in writing from right to left his writing hand would always pass over the part of the page with no writing yet on it. His assistants were likely (statistically speaking and given the evidence) to be right-handed and so would not have this advantage. In fact, it is believed that Leonardo may have adopted mirrored writing to overcome this exact problem.

Leonardo's Robot 33
The mid-length cable is the green cable, which also caused the knight to stand. Similarly, the shortest cable is the yellow cable, which caused the knight to raise its arms; and the longest cable is the red cable, which caused the knight to sit.

The Panel Problem 34

There were 42 different rectangles that could be formed—not all simultaneously, of course, however.

Cubic Question 36

There are 38 cubes: 18 on the bottom layer, then 14 on the next, then 5 on the one above, and then finally a single cube on the uppermost layer.

Flying Bicycle 37

Because then it would have been a flying tricycle.

Perfect Match 38

30 matchsticks. Although the shape consists of 20 triangular faces, each edge on the final 3D shape is shared with the edge of another face, meaning there are only half as many edges as one might initially think. In order to build a model, therefore, Leonardo would only need 30 matchsticks—one for each edge. (Or, if you prefer, 27 matchsticks if you accept that he already had the 3 described in the text.)

Caught in the Net 40

Net 4 is the only one which could be used to make the complete octahedron.

All at Sea 43

He had been attempting to design a submarine—which was therefore *supposed* to sink below the surface of the water.

A Dicey Game 1 44

Roll 1: 1.

Roll 2: 3.

Roll 3: 4.

Roll 4: 5.

Roll 5: 6.

Roll 6: 2.

Number Sets 1 45

He had put the prime numbers into set 2, then placed the remaining evens into set 1, and the odds into set 3.

Unfriendly Fire 47

19 seconds. The first fuse would be lit at 0 seconds on a hypothetical clock, the second at 1 second, the third at 2 seconds, and so on, until the final fuse was lit 19 seconds after the first.

Future Improvements 48

A (12-hour) clock. For example, if you add 4 hours onto 9 (am), you end up with 1 (pm), and so on.

Family Values 49

Seven children: four daughters and three sons.

How Many Hulls? 50

The *Iota*. It had two hulls and covered six yards with a cargo of shoes.

Meanwhile, the *Delta* had three hulls and went a distance of four yards with a cargo of paintbrushes. The *Zeta* had one hull, and progressed only three yards with a cargo of books.

Code Conundrum 51

The code was: **81018**

Proportional Representation 52

The man would have been 168 cm tall, and his feet 24 cm long.

NB These are the real proportions suggested by Leonardo in his *Vitruvian Man*.

The Water Test 54

Fill the 3-gallon vessel and pour it into the 7-gallon vessel twice. Then fill up the 3-gallon vessel a third time and use it to fill the remaining 1 gallon of space in the 7-gallon vessel. With 2 gallons left in the 3-gallon vessel, empty the 7-gallon vessel and pour the 2 gallons into it, then fill the 3-gallon vessel for a final time and pour it into the 7-gallon vessel to result in a measurement of exactly 5 gallons.

Structural Query.. 55

The courtyard and gallery would each have an area of 36 square yards, and the gallery a width of 4 yards.

Sleep Cycle.. 57

58 hours. On a modern calendar, there is only one month which can start and end on the same day: February during a leap year. Sleeping for 20 minutes every four hours gives a total of two hours of sleep in every 24-hour period, and multiplying this by 29 (the number of days in a leap February) gives a total of 58 hours.

NB This is actually a sleeping pattern that Leonardo was famous for.

The Ideal City.. 58

On the sixth day, he would draw 13 buildings. He was drawing them according to the sequence of prime numbers: he drew 2 buildings on the first day, then 3, 5, 7, 11, and (on the sixth day) 13.

Planning Problem... 59

600 yards. Leonardo took 140 strides + 160 strides *plus* an unknown distance to reach the square. On the way back, he walked 140 strides + 160 strides *minus* an unknown distance. The unknown distances therefore cancel out, and overall he walked a total of 600 strides = 600 yards.

What's *not* possible to calculate from the numbers given is the distance from the city gate to the main square with no detour.

The Uncommon Clock.. 60

The clock had Roman numerals on its face, so "I" looked like "1", and "ll" looked like "11", although it in fact represented "2"—just an hour later.

The Hidden Agenda... 61

"Today" and "tomorrow".

No Neutral Tones.. 62

The pieces for a chess set. Each had made a full set of pieces in a different hue.

NB Apparently Leonardo may *really* have had a hand in the design of the modern chess set.

The Coin Conundrum 63

By placing the silver coins in a closed circle, and then placing the gold coin on top:

Paintbrush Positions... 64

The pupils would need to create a 3D structure with the handles, arranging them into a triangular-based pyramid. This would have an equilateral triangle for all four faces, despite having only six edges.

Pigment Problem 65

Half a pint. The volume of pigment has not changed but now constitutes 2 percent of the overall volume, so the overall volume must have halved.

Instrumental Notes 66

The first letters of each name correspond to the traditional names of musical notes: DOmenico, REnato, MIchelangelo, FAbrizio, SOfia, LAura. But "Silvio" does not begin with a musical note, so this is the odd one out.

The Moon and its Moods 69

The full moon was recorded from the university rooftop at midnight. Also, the half-moon was recorded at 2 am from the workshop rooftop, and the new moon was recorded at 10 pm from the basilica rooftop.

The Pay Rise.. 70

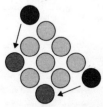

Just two. Leonardo could move the coins shaded in black into the positions shown in order to create a 3 x 3 square.

The Arm Spans.. 71

In order of their being measured, the arm spans of the apprentices were as follows:

1. Franco: 124 cm.
2. Giulio: 123 cm.
3. Matteo: 142 cm.
4. Pietro: 125 cm.
5. Cosimo: 144 cm.

Masterpiece Mix-Up 72

La Gioconda—known in English as the *Mona Lisa*. The paintings were created in the following order, from earliest to latest:

1. *Ginevra de' Benci.*

2. *Portrait of a Musician.*

3. *Lady with an Ermine.*

4. *La Belle Ferronnière.*

5. *La Gioconda.*

NB This is the real order of creation of these paintings—if Leonardo did indeed personally paint them all.

Time and Time Again 74

6 am.

Benevolent Benefactors 75

Leonardo had 44 brushes to begin with:

• Giacomo took 24.

• Ambrogio took 6.

• Bernardino took 5.

• Cesare took 4.

• Martino took the remaining 5.

The Bonus 76

One of the apprentices was given the pouch with the final coin still inside it.

A Loaded Question 77

The heavier block would be 64 times heavier than the smaller one, since the volume will be 4^3 = 4x4x4 times larger if all dimensions become 4x greater. A 1x1x1 inch cube, for example, would have a volume of 1 inch cubed, but a 4x4x4 inch cube would have a volume of 64 inches cubed.

Rescue Mission 78

Leonardo could have his apprentice hold one end of the rope and stand on the shore of the lake. Then, holding the other end of the rope, he could walk around the shore of the circular lake, keeping the rope below the level of the boat's central mast. When he returned to his apprentice, the rope would be wrapped around the mast, and the two could pull it back to the edge of the lake.

Fetch and Carry 79

Giacomo had done more of the carrying—10 miles more.

The Military Model 80

28 cannons. The smaller model had 24 mounts, and the larger one had 36.

Weighty Decisions 83

42 g. Both silver coins are the same weight, so can be removed from the equation. Removing these shows that three bronze coins are equivalent to one bronze and one gold coin. Remove a bronze coin from each side, and one gold coin is clearly the weight of two bronze coins.

The Test of Time... 84

A sundial and an hourglass.

Clay Figures 85

36 blocks. This accounts for an initial 36 statues, 12 to be made from the leftovers, then 4 from the leftovers of the 12. Of the final four statues, the remainders of three could be made into a final block, resulting in one more statue and an additional third of a block. Adding to this the third remaining from the fourth of the final four statues would mean two-thirds of a block remaining at the end—which, it can be worked out, is exactly the amount of clay needed for a final (54th) sculpture.

The Scale of Things 1 86

2.7 km—i.e. 18 cm x 3/2 x 10,000.

The Throwaway Design 88

A parachute.

Shades of Shades 89

17. This is equal to 1+2+3+4+5+...+16+17.

Watching the Clock.. 90

The minute and hour hands had been swapped, so what should appear as 2:15 appeared as 3:10, and what should appear as 4:15 appeared as 3:20.

The Supper Sketches 93

27 sketches of Judas. He had also drawn 12 of Peter and 9 of John.

The Scale of Things 2 94

It is a certainty, assuming that every position on each map is considered as a location.

The Wingspans.. 97

From largest to smallest:

- Eagle: 100 cm.
- Kite: 60 cm.
- Thrush: 35 cm.
- Lark: 30 cm.
- Sparrow: 20 cm.

NB Leonardo did prepare for his flying machine by studying birds, and these are their real typical wingspans.

Taking Stock.. 98

Eight of them had oil paint. Three had chalk, four had pencil, and twenty had water-based paint.

Inky Issues 99

Ten weeks (i.e. 10+9+8+7+...+2+1 weeks).

Solar Solution... 100

A sundial.

Walking on Water 2 103

1 minute. If he swam back from the middle in 1.5 minutes but this was a third of the speed of the walking device, then he must have taken only 0.5 minutes to reach the midpoint using the device. Therefore, it would have taken him only 1 minute to cross the entire lake while using it.

Turn the Time 104

He should turn over the 2-minute and the 5-minute hourglasses at the same time. When the 2-minute hourglass runs out, he should start the steam-powered device. Then, when the 5-minute hourglass runs out (which will therefore be 3 minutes after starting the device), he should turn over the 7-minute hourglass. When all the sand has run through this final hourglass, he will have measured out the full 10 minutes.

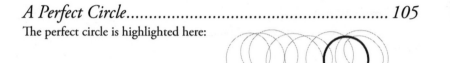

A Perfect Circle.. *105*

The perfect circle is highlighted here:

Apprentice Appraisal.................................... *106*

Stefano. In order of being seen by Leonardo, the candidates were Luca, Giovanni, Francesco, Stefano, and then Alessandro.

A Dicey Game 2.. *109*

In order, the rolls were 6, 5, 2, 1, 3, 4. Therefore Leonardo's prediction was not correct.

Figuratively Speaking................................... *110*

From left to right:

- The first image would feature Mary, be predominantly blue, and be painted by Angelo.

- The second image would feature Michael, be predominantly red, and be painted by Antonio.

- The third image would feature Saint John, be predominantly green, and be painted by Lorenzo.

- The fourth image would feature Saint Mark, be predominantly orange, and be painted by Marco.

The Mirror Link.. *113*

Sculptural Challenge................................... *114*

The horse on the left of the painting was sculpted from wax in a bucking pose. Meanwhile, the horse sculpted from clay, in a galloping pose, would be in the middle of the painting, and the horse sculpted from plaster, in a standing pose, would be on the right of the painting.

A Dicey Game 3 116

In order, his six rolls were 5, 2, 3, 2, 1, 4.

The Cover of Darkness............................... 117

7:39 pm (and 44 seconds, so you might also say 7:40 pm). The fifth Sunday would be four Sundays later, so would be 4 x 7 = 28 days later. Now, 28 x 128 seconds (i.e. 2 minutes, 8 seconds) = 3,584 seconds = 59 minutes and 44 seconds later.

Signature Sketch 118

The differences in each signature are circled below:

ℓ.Dₐ Ⓥnci ₁₅₀₇

ℓ.Dₐ Vn©i ₁₅₀₇

ℓ.Ⓓₐ Vnci ₁₅₀₇

ℓ.Dₐ Vn©₁₅₀₇

Not Born Yesterday 120

1452.

Dizzy Heights... 121

Luca was 164 cm, Mauro 171 cm, and Giorgio 182 cm. The difference in height between the shortest and tallest was 18 cm.

Aerial View 1 122

C is the only option that could be a bird's-eye view of the building.

NB Leonardo really did draw an accurate map of Imola—apparently so accurate that you could still use it to navigate the city today.

Get in Gear... 124

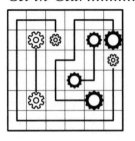

NB Leonardo did actually design a hoisting device with gear wheels and a pulley system.

The Apprentice's Graduation 126

The image he had created was an optical illusion. If you cover the outer gradations, you will see that the central bar is a single, solid shade from top to bottom.

Abandoned Works 128

Cecilia. Her sketch was made with oils and had a background of cypress trees. Beatrice's sketch was made with pastel and had a background of pine trees, while Lucretia's sketch was made with ink and had a background of olive trees.

Geared Up 1 131

Gear B would spin counterclockwise.

The Draw.. 132

30 sketches (i.e. 16 + 8 + 4 + 2).

Age is Just a Number.. 133

Aldo was paid 28 coins, Ottavio was paid 24 coins, and Dante was paid 21 coins.

A State of Amazement.. 134

NB Many fortified cities were built in hexagonal shapes.

The Head Start.. 137

Neither—they would draw level exactly at the finish line. The slower machine would take 30 seconds to reach the end of the race, and the faster one would take 24 seconds. With a 6-second delay, they would cross the line at the same time.

Pulley the Other One 138

The Water Fountains.. *140*

The fountains must be placed in the locations indicated with stars.

Ahead of his Time... *142*

45.

Multi-Faceted Problem... *143*

36 sides.

Aerial View 2... *144*

E is the only option that could be a bird's-eye view of the building.

To Coin a Phrase.. *146*

He had two gold coins. He would then be due change for buying just five pots of pigment with it.

Time and Dedication.. *147*

36 pages.

Triangulation Problem.. *149*

There are 28 quadrilaterals and 10 triangles.

Exploded View 1.. *150*

Only Cesare's drawing could create the top arrangement with no extra parts.

Chalk It Up *152*

6/16 = 3/8 = 0.375 = 37.5%. If B is black chalk, and R is red chalk, then there are six possible ways of filling the box with equal numbers of each: BBRR, BRBR, BRRB, RBBR, RBRB and RRBB. Overall there are sixteen ways of filling the box with any combination of chalk, so the likelihood is 6/16.

Out of all Proportion *153*

80 cm.

Exploded View 2 154

Only Dante's drawing could create the top arrangement with the pieces as shown.

Secret Sketches 156

The mistress's name was Cecilia Gallerani. Letters in both names have been replaced by letters in the "opposite" position in the alphabet—that is, A has been replaced with Z, B replaced with Y, and so on, until Y is replaced with B, and Z is replaced with A. This is known as an "Atbash" cipher.

Clearing Out 157

20.

Pots and Lids 158

The Family Tree Fee 161

Six cold coins. The family tree could consist of one man, his two sons, their only sons, and one of those son's sons.

Strange Sum Sequence 162

The final number should be 9. In each of the previous numbers, the digits have been added together to form a sum; and then if that sum has more than one digits, *those* digits have been added together again; and so on, until a single digit emerges.

- $9 + 9 + 9 + 9 = 36; 3 + 6 = 9$
- $8 + 8 + 8 + 8 = 32; 3 + 2 = 5$
- $7 + 7 + 7 + 7 = 28; 2 + 8 = 10, 1 + 0 = 1$
- $6 + 6 + 6 + 6 = 24; 2 + 4 = 6$
- $9 + 9 + 9 = 27; 2 + 7 = 9$
- $8 + 8 + 8 = 24; 2 + 4 = 6$
- $7 + 7 + 7 = 21; 2 + 1 = 3$
- $6 + 6 + 6 = 18; 1 + 8 = 9$

Number Sets 2 163

Set 1: Square numbers.

Set 2: Overlap of sets 1 and 3.

Set 3: Cube numbers.

Silver Areas 164

All of the circles were pure white. The appearance of apparently silver circles is an illusion created by the contrast between the black and white areas of the image.

Flight Pattern 166

It would take longer for the bird to make the ten round-trips if the wind was blowing than if it was not. Although it seems that the head and tailwinds should cancel one another out, the headwind acts on the bird for a greater amount of time because it slows the bird down, just as the tailwind benefits the bird for less time because it speeds the bird up—so the overall effect means the combined journeys take longer.

The Outposts 168

The cannons must be placed in the locations indicated with stars.

Connections Conundrum 1 170

Set A: Planets in the solar system.

Set A+B: Planets in the solar system that share their name with Roman gods and goddesses.

Set B: Roman gods and goddesses.

The Whole Dam Problem 171

The water would still need to flow somewhere, dam or not, and building a dam immediately west of Florence might also flood Florence, thus destroying the city.

NB Leonardo really did come up with plans to divert the course of the Arno after it had flowed through Florence, but the engineers didn't follow his plans accurately and the scheme literally collapsed.

Geared Up 2 172
The bridge was being raised, as gear A would be turning counterclockwise.

Into the Fold 175
The *Mona Lisa*, the name given to the portrait in English, is painted on a wooden plank—so it cannot be folded or rolled.

Exploded View 3 176
Only Cesare's drawing could create the arrangement on the left with no extra pieces.

Number Sets 3 177
Set 1: Digits drawn using only curved lines.

Set 2: Digits drawn with a mixture of curved and straight lines.

Set 3: Digits drawn using only straight lines.

The Longest Night 178
On the longest night of the year, in December, a stream might well be frozen over, so a bridge would not be necessary.

Order of Magnitude 179
27 pots of red ink. Overall, there were three boxes of red ink and five of black ink, giving him 27 red pots and 35 black pots.

Aerial View 3 180
B is the only option that could be a bird's-eye view of the building.

The Missing Coins 182
Leonardo explained that they were mistaken: there were no missing coins. Consider the final physical locations of the actual coins: each of the three apprentices had one, the waiter had one, and the remaining coins were at the tavern. Take four away from the original eighteen that they handed over—as the proprietor did—and there were only fourteen coins at the tavern.

Frame of Mind 183
He needed to cut 10 inches from the angled plank, to make it 40 inches in length. The measurement can be worked out with Pythagoras' theorem.

Blue Period *184*

He had started with 72 pots. He used 36 in the first month, 18 in the second month, 6 in the third month, and then was left with 12 pots (one-sixth of 72).

Spring into Action *186*

If it moved exactly as described, it would never travel over 2 yards. As the distance halved every second, the distance would rapidly approach 2 yards but never quite reach it—or pass it.

The Great Divide *187*

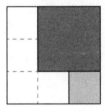

The two older apprentices should cover 4 square yards each, and the youngest 1 square yard. Splitting the 9 square yard area into nine smaller squares of 1 square yard each, one of many possible solutions is as follows, where the top-right shaded square could be covered by the oldest apprentice, the bottom-right square by the youngest, and the rest by the remaining apprentice.

Divisions, Decisions *188*

One apprentice should draw a line to divide the desk in half in whichever way he saw fit, and then the second apprentice should choose the half he would prefer. In that way, there is no incentive for the first apprentice to split the space unevenly, as they are likely to be left with the smaller "half".

Weights and Measures *189*

Just two. He should start by splitting the bars into three groups of three. Weighing two of these groups will determine which group the underweight bar is in: if it's one of the two on the scales, then they will tip, with the group containing the underweight bar rising higher than the other—or if the two groups are identical in weight, then it must be the group not weighed that contains the lighter bar. Leonardo can then take the three bars from this group and weigh one of them against the other—if the scales tip, then the higher of the two is the light bar. If the scales do not tip, the remaining bar from the group must be the light one.

Open Air *190*

The piazzas must be placed in the locations indicated with stars.